Managing Editor
Mara Ellen Guckian

Editor in Chief
Karen J. Goldfluss, M.S. Ed.

Creative Director
Sarah M. Fournier

Cover Artist
Diem Pascarella

Illustrator
Mark Mason

Art Coordinator
Renée Mc Elwee

Imaging
Amanda R. Harter

Publisher
Mary D. Smith, M.S. Ed.

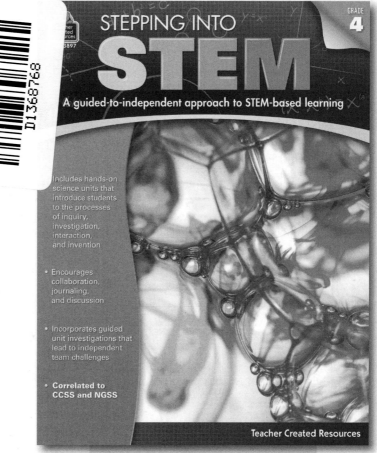

GRADE 4

STEPPING INTO STEM

A guided-to-independent approach to STEM-based learning

Includes hands-on science units that introduce students to the processes of inquiry, investigation, interaction, and invention

- Encourages collaboration, journaling, and discussion

- Incorporates guided unit investigations that lead to independent team challenges

- Correlated to CCSS and NGSS

Teacher Created Resources

Author
Robert Smith

CORRELATED TO **CCSS & NGSS**

For correlations to the Common Core State Standards, see pages 158–159 of this book or visit *http://www.teachercreated.com/standards/*. For correlations to the Next Generation Science Standards, see page 160.

Teacher Created Resources

12621 Western Avenue

Garden Grove, CA 92841

www.teachercreated.com

ISBN: 978-1-4206-3897-4

©2016 Teacher Created Resources

Made in U.S.A.

Teacher Created Resources

C-O-N-T-E-N-T-S

Introduction

Project-based Learning

As educators, we are being required to place more emphasis on science, technology, engineering, and math (STEM) to ensure that today's students will be prepared for their future careers. Additionally, it is important that children learn and practice the 21st-century skills of collaboration, critical thinking, problem solving, and digital literacy in their daily curricula. It is imperative that students learn these collaborative skills, but acquiring these skills is not without challenge. *Stepping into STEM* provides students with needed practice in these areas.

Project-based learning, simply put, is learning by doing. Project-based learning, or PBL, tends to be deeper learning that is more relevant to students, and thus remembered longer. We need to educate students to be global competitors, and to do so, we must help them to think creatively, take risks, and put what they are learning into practice. After all, it doesn't do much good to know a formula if you don't know when to use it. Students also need to learn the value of failure as a learning experience. Some of the ideas and efforts made during an activity will not work. This can turn into a very positive experience since knowing what won't work, and why, can possibly lead to the discovery of what will work!

Reading informational material provides needed background, but *doing* makes the difference. Concepts, ideas, and experiences of hands-on activities remain lodged in the brain for retrieval when needed.

In STEM curriculum, project-based learning is a must! Its collaborative style guarantees that 21st-century skills are fully integrated into the curriculum while supporting students' academic and socio-emotional growth. Furthermore, PBL allows teachers to immediately assess what students comprehend, then adapt curriculum accordingly.

Connecting Science, Technology, Engineering, and Math

STEM activities blend science and engineering learning experiences. Technology—both simple and high-tech—provides the framework for recording information. Phones, tablets, and computers are effective in recording and comparing activity results. The math element might involve sequencing, patterns, or recognizing shapes, size, and volume. Comparisons are expressed in decimals, fractions, ratios, and percentages, as well as measurements, graphs, charts, and other visual representations.

The Need for Interaction and Collaboration

Today's scientists and engineers share ideas, experiments, and solutions—as well as failures—with colleagues around the globe. Student scientists and engineers, like their professional counterparts, need experience working with partners while in a collaborative and supportive environment. They need to exchange ideas, test theories, perform experiments, modify their experiments, try novel approaches—even those that may not appear useful or serious—and cooperate with each other in all aspects of the project as they seek to accomplish their objective.

Successful teams are able to work together and be respectful even when they disagree. Each team member must be responsible and accountable for his or her part of the work. Depending upon the activity, students may use the Design Process or the Scientific Method in order to accomplish their objective.

A basic requirement of these collaborative efforts is a willingness to seriously consider all suggestions from the members of the team. Ideas should be considered, tried, tested, and compared for use in the project. Students should work together to select the most efficient and practical ideas, then methodically test each one for its useful application in the activity.

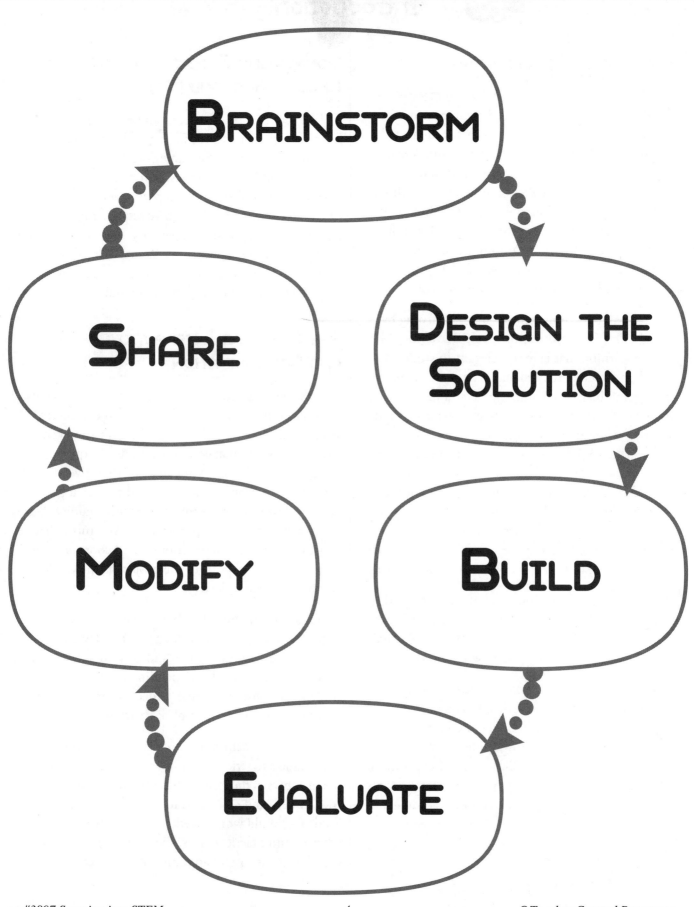

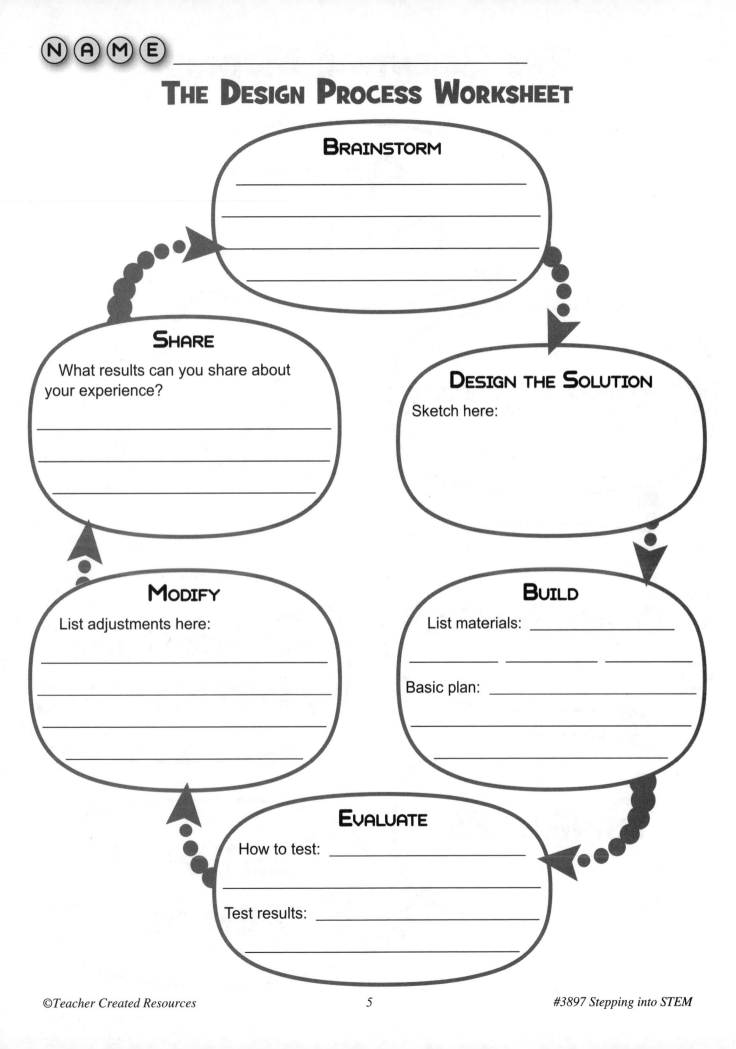

NAME _____

THE DESIGN PROCESS WORKSHEET

BRAINSTORM

_____

_____

_____

_____

SHARE

What results can you share about your experience?

_____

_____

_____

DESIGN THE SOLUTION

Sketch here:

MODIFY

List adjustments here:

_____

_____

_____

_____

BUILD

List materials: _____

_____ _____ _____

Basic plan: _____

_____

_____

EVALUATE

How to test: _____

_____

Test results: _____

_____

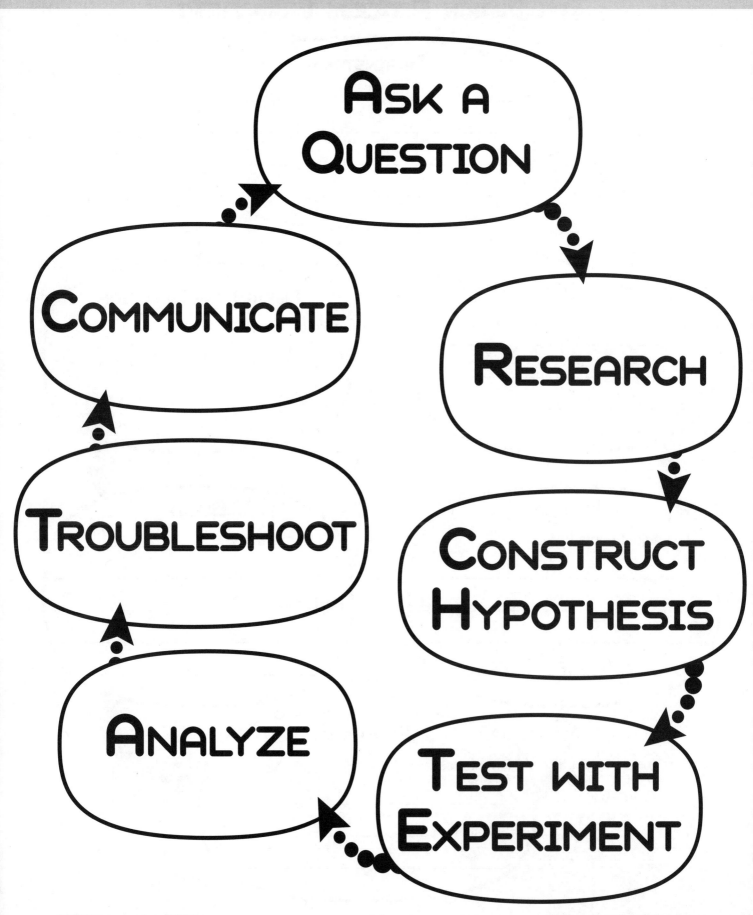

THE SCIENTIFIC METHOD WORKSHEET

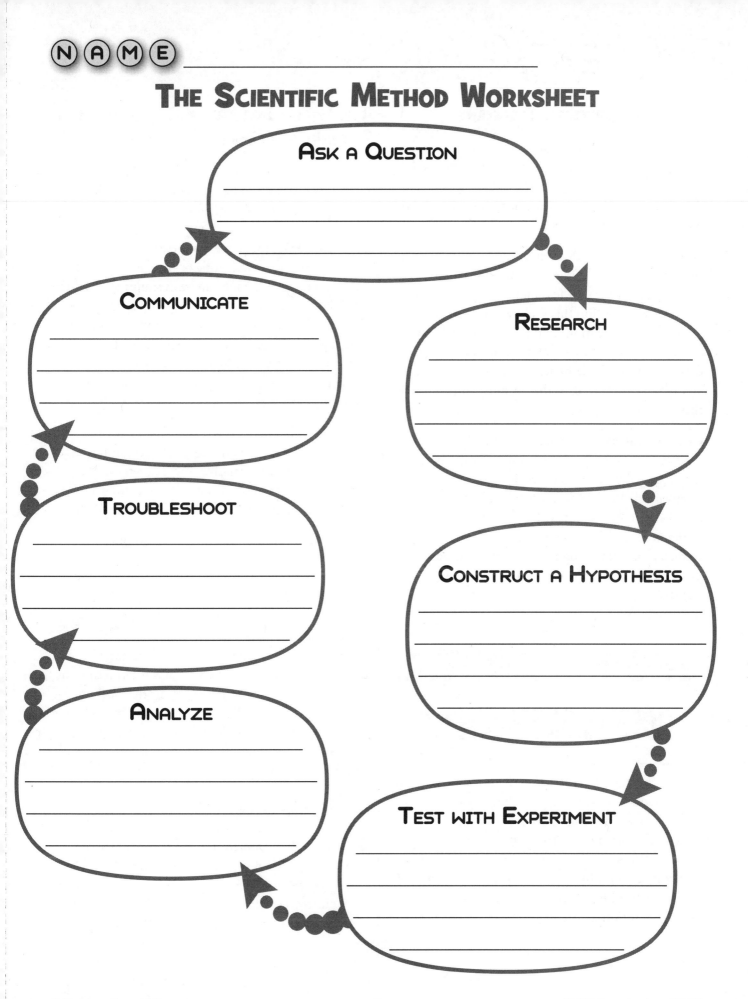

ASK A QUESTION

COMMUNICATE

RESEARCH

TROUBLESHOOT

CONSTRUCT A HYPOTHESIS

ANALYZE

TEST WITH EXPERIMENT

GROWING CRITICAL THINKERS

While all members of a team need to be respected and heard, members of the team also need to critically examine each idea to see if it is feasible. This is part of the design process, used by engineers, and the scientific method, employed by scientists.

Students need to apply their learned experiences in these activities, and serious attention should be given to testing each idea for feasibility and practicality. Students can develop this skill by considering each serious suggestion, testing it for workability, and then determining its value. Students need to examine the available materials, work with them in an organized way, record their results, and compare these results.

Critical thinkers are organized and methodical in their testing and experimentation. They examine the ideas generated in the free flow of comments and discussions. They determine which ideas can be tested and then carefully compared for useful application to the problem. They keep open minds. Critical thinkers base their judgments on observations and proven outcomes. Critical thinkers aren't negative, but they are skeptical until they observe the results of an activity.

> "Show me." "Let's check it out."

> "How can we test it to see if it works?"

One of the hallmarks of a scientist is the inclination to ask questions. Another is making the effort to seek answers through effective investigations, tests, and experiments. You want to encourage your student scientists to practice critical thinking by asking thoughtful questions using academic vocabulary and by developing creative ways to test possible solutions.

THE 4 *I*s: INQUIRE • INVESTIGATE • INTERACT • INVENT

The four basic elements of an effective science or STEM activity can be categorized as Inquiry, Investigation, Interaction, and Invention.

1. INQUIRY is the process of determining what you wish to learn about a scientific or natural phenomenon. The natural phenomenon can be as simple as watching a swing moving back and forth, a schoolyard game of marbles, or sucking on a straw. Some of the same principles of science may apply to a helicopter rescue of a swimmer, a batted ball in a major-league game, or the process of getting water out of a ditch. The questions are always the same:

"Why did it happen? Will it happen every time? What happens if . . . you change the length of the swing, the size of the marble, the diameter of the straw, the weight of the swimmer, the diameter of the ball, or the length of the siphon hose in the ditch?"

In the simplest form, **Inquire** is a question: Why . . . ?, What if . . . ?, How . . . ?

2. INVESTIGATION is the action a scientist takes to learn more about the question. It involves the process a student scientist needs to follow. The investigation can involve background research, the process of doing an experiment, and interpreting the results. Reading a science text about the workings of the pendulum is not the same as actually constructing a working pendulum, adjusting it to different lengths and weights, and carefully observing its features and behaviors in varying circumstances. Measuring these things in mathematical terms provides the opportunity for valid comparisons as well.

3. INTERACTION requires student scientists to collaborate with one or more classmates. Together they assess the problem or question, determine and carry out the investigation, and analyze the results.

From a practical point of view, experiments done with students are more effective with teams of two. In larger groups, one or more team members often feel left out, don't get to actually do the hands-on construction, and can end up engaging in distracting behaviors. Teams of two require the active involvement of both individuals in all phases of the activity, all the time. The one off-task student in a team can be refocused by a partner or the teacher.

It is important to have enough materials and equipment for each team's basic activity. The materials used in the activities in this book are inexpensive and easily available to facilitate two-person teams.

4. INVENTION is the final stage of the 4 *I*s in a science activity, i.e., the effort to create or invent a solution, modification, or improvement. This can be the most challenging aspect of the activity. At first, suggestions tend to be far out, impractical, silly, or impossible to realize with the available materials. The most effective teams discuss possible solutions and then start manipulating the materials as a form of "thinking with their hands."

The invention aspect of the activity is nearly always the final step of the activity. For instance, after multiple sessions manipulating and measuring results with a pendulum, students should have enough background and hands-on experience to invent an application for this tool. It may be a toy swing for a doll, a time-keeping mechanism for a class activity such as a timed math-facts sheet, or an attempt to make a perpetual motion machine (or one that just lasts longer than anybody else's).

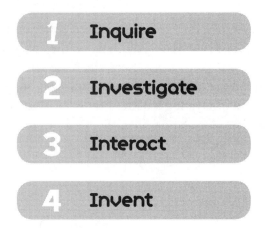

1 Inquire

2 Investigate

3 Interact

4 Invent

THE NEED FOR JOURNALING

Scientists keep records. They are meticulous in recording the results of their investigations and often refer back to investigations done in previous months and years. They use this information as needed for further investigations, related experiments, and in publishing their work.

Ideally, all students should keep journals recording the investigations on which they have been working. With continued practice, students will develop the habit of journaling after each period of investigation. It is easier for students to keep information in one place and to refer back to previous investigations for discussion and record-keeping purposes. Consider having students use 3-ring binders to keep unit pages together with additional notes, ideas, and sketches.

It is suggested that a separate entry be made for each investigation session. Have students enter the date and investigation title for each new entry. Include a key question for each activity. This is the starting point for each investigation. As students proceed, they should record, using adequate details, the process and materials used to investigate the question. Encourage students to use appropriate vocabulary when journaling.

The variations in technique, the engineering adjustments, the technology employed, and the results of each modification should be recorded. The mathematical applications should also be noted. If the length of the pendulum fishing line was doubled or cut in half, this is critical information. If the weight was doubled from 8 grams to 16 grams, it should be noted, and then the effect on the pendulum's swing distance and duration should be recorded. There should be a record of each trial.

The most important information in the journal should be the research teams' conclusions about the testable questions the team was investigating. Individual researchers may draw separate conclusions about these questions, but the conclusions need to be based on objective facts and recorded information.

THE REVIEW DISCUSSIONS

The journal entries should be the "notes" student scientists use when sharing their information during each class review discussion. Either the *Design Process* or the *Scientific Method* can be used, depending on the topic. The teacher acts as the moderator of these discussions and should ensure that each student gets an opportunity to share his or her experiences, results, and scientific observations. These discussions work well as 10-minute closure activities at the end of each period.

Encourage all students to take turns sharing the results of their activities and the conclusions they drew from their experiments. Data summaries may include photos, videos, or other relevant materials.

Model and encourage serious reporting. Encourage students to incorporate new vocabulary into their discussions, their journaling, and their presentation pieces.

The writing (journaling) and the review are vital elements in the design process. They provide students with the opportunity to share their experiences, and they serve as excellent parts of the assessment process. It is suggested that you allow at least 20 minutes to complete these activities.

You may choose to act as moderator. You can allow students to share as teams or as individuals about each activity and other activities they have done on related subjects. You may also use smaller groups with student moderators.

KEEPING THINGS IN PERSPECTIVE!

A STEM class will rarely be perfectly quiet! In fact, the low buzz of purposeful conversation is an indicator that students are actively engaged. The teacher serves as the facilitator, providing guidance, crucial information, and directions at the outset. It is important to regularly check on each group to offer encouragement, advice, correction, and support.

Teachers need to evaluate how students are doing as teams proceed with investigations. In addition to guiding the learning process, it is also very important to draw closure on the activity by moderating the final portion of the *Design Process Review* in which you draw conclusions and highlight the core learning concepts embedded in the activity.

Unsuccessful periods happen in any kind of class, no matter how capable the instructor or how gifted the class. Myriad things can go wrong—announcements from the intercom break the flow of instruction and construction, an activity can go awry, or one of countless other distractions of school life can occur. You may get a true scientific discussion going, but have it go off into areas unrelated to the thrust of the investigation.

But there are also those times when you encounter the pleasant experience of no one paying any attention to the distraction. A visitor or principal enters the room, observes the activity for a moment, and either leaves or joins a group. The science discussion reverts to the main idea and goes smoothly or vigorously along, driven by students who are focused and on task. Yes, it happens!

Students can really "get into" science. They enjoy the openness involved in the activity, the collegial nature of working on a project, the materials they get to manipulate, and the mental stimulation of solving a problem or creating a better product. A good, productive, stimulating science period can make their day—and yours, too.

How to Use This Book

Stepping into STEM is arranged with flexibility in mind. One method is to move from lesson to lesson in each unit and proceed through the units in order. However, the number and order of units completed throughout the year is completely dependent on classroom and curriculum needs. You may want to choose the activities with which you are more familiar or those that fit your school schedule better. The organization of each unit moves from teacher-directed activities, to more student-driven activities, to a final challenge activity which allows students to create their own unique products or inventions. Students should be encouraged to follow the Design Process while doing the activities in each unit.

PACING UNITS AND LESSONS

The amount of time alloted for completion of each unit can be flexible. You may choose to utilize some or all of the units and can intersperse them throughout the year, incorporating each unit into your science curriculum. If a unit topic fits in well with what is currently being taught, embed it into the schedule where possible. Since these unit investigations were developed to foster a STEM approach to learning, they do not have to be tied to any specific time frame or subject in the science curriculum.

To get the most out of a unit, it is suggested that a few sessions be allotted to complete the activities. These can be spread out as needed. Usually, an activity can be done in about an hour. For those fortunate enough to have a one-and-a-half hour period, students will have more time to explore the variations in each project and to extend their creative explorations. Remember that the unit activities can be broken into more than one session! Be sure to allow focused time for journaling and recording information in each period.

VOCABULARY AND DISCUSSIONS

Share and discuss the STEM Vocabulary List (page 17) and unit vocabulary lists with students. Identify and use the terms frequently throughout the sessions in order to reinforce essential subject-area vocabulary. Enlarge each unit list in order to create posters for student reference, or photocopy a list for each student to keep in his or her journaling notebook.

Encourage discussions within groups and between groups as long as they are focused on the topic. At the end of each activity, allow time for the teacher- or student-moderated review activities, in which individuals share their experiments, designs, results, and conclusions based on their research.

A general activity period could allow 5 to 7 minutes for teacher introduction and review of previous learning, 5 minutes to efficiently distribute supplies, and 30 to 40 minutes to complete the activity involving science, technology, engineering, and math. The remaining time should be devoted to science journaling.

TEACHER AND STUDENT RUBRICS

Use the teacher rubric on page 18 to evaluate team progress, time-on-task, student interaction, and to reinforce STEM objectives. Students who are focused on the objective and methodically trying different ways to solve a problem are doing science. So are those who are responding a bit randomly to their own ideas and trying them out.

As student groups work through each investigation, they should complete the student rubric on page 19 in order to reinforce the processes they used and to reflect on the procedures they followed.

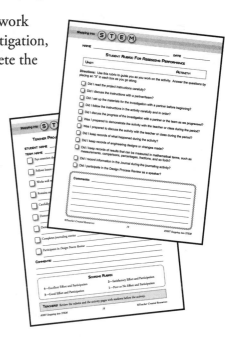

NOTE: Explain both rubrics to students before starting the units. It is important for them to know how their work will be evaluated and what steps they should follow as they work on a unit investigation.

CHALLENGE ACTIVITY

Each of the units culminates in a challenge assignment. Students are asked to create a new version of a product or to extend experimentation based on the activities in the unit. Students are advised to look over their journals and other documentation collected during the unit and to pick an extension. They are to use either the Design Process to create something new, or the Scientific Method, in which nature and how it works is the focus. The choice of method used will be determined by the objective of the assignment and whether engineering or science will be the focus. Opportunities for both are provided in this book.

For example, students doing the Centripetal Force unit make lifting spinners first and later water spinners. They observe which vessels carry the biggest and most balanced loads. They learn the advantages of different motions and the advantages of different weights. Students then use the Design Process as a guide for the challenge assignment to build spinners of their own design using materials from the unit.

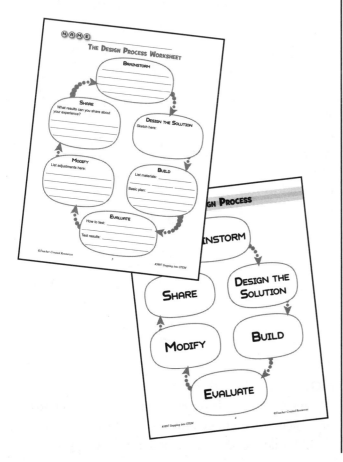

The Scientific Method is used when students approach a culminating challenge activity with more emphasis on science—as they do in the unit Surface Tension. Here, the emphasis is not on building (engineering) but on testing a hypothesis about ingredients and what might happen when they are mixed.

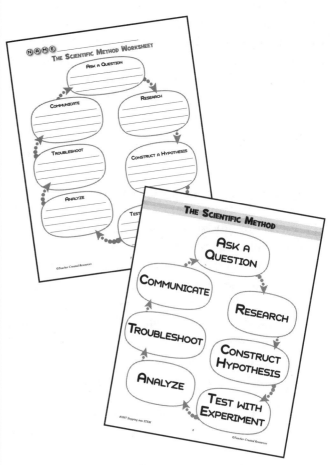

Allow time for imagination, frustration, and revamping during the building and testing periods of the challenge assignments. Use the grading rubric to evaluate creativity, success, effort, and on-task work time.

TEAM MANAGEMENT

The activities in this series were designed to maximize student participation. Students will work in pairs or small collaborative teams. The collaborative process is essential to construct the apparatus and create the models. Four hands and two minds working together are more efficient and effective than individuals proceeding alone.

Lesson Notes for the Teacher

LESSON 1—GUIDED ACTIVITY

The first lesson is designed so that the teacher can guide and control the pace of the activity and can ensure that students know how to function in this type of science activity and with these materials. It is more teacher-directed in terms of time and following specific directions than later lessons in the unit.

Providing guidance through the beginning phases of each unit will set the stage for student groups to continue with their investigations and discussions throughout the units. This is also an opportunity for the teacher to note which teams or students might be struggling and to provide more assistance to them.

LESSONS—YOUR TURN

Review students' findings and ideas related to their investigations in Activity 1. Discuss how students will be exploring how a project works under various conditions. This can be an independent collaborative group activity. Students work in pairs.

The next two or three lessons allow students to work at their own paces as they do the activities. The teacher circulates through the room giving advice, encouragement, and correction as needed. Students work in pairs.

Get ready!

FINAL LESSON—THE CHALLENGE

The final lesson in each unit involves a Challenge Activity in which students apply what they have learned in earlier lessons in order to to solve a specific problem or to make the fastest, best, or most unique application of the concepts learned. Students should work in pairs.

ABOUT TEAMS

Although there are always students who prefer to work alone—and have difficulty working with others—most students quickly find that these projects need 3 or 4 hands working in unison to work well. Most students also realize that the opportunity to share ideas and experiences helps their own performance and is reflected in their success in a project.

You may want to have students switch partners when you start a new unit or after partners have been together for a few units.

Whenever possible, keep the teams small (two people) and therefore more likely to keep their hands and minds occupied and on task.

The activities in this series are designed for full participation by all students with all students actively engaged at all times. All students will use the materials and should have access to the necessary equipment. Students work in collaborative teams in order to facilitate learning, but all students are actively engaged with all aspects of the projects.

There are very few lone scientists working in private anymore in this age of scientific and technological discovery. Teamwork matters—kinesthetic experiences and collaborative interaction with peers are essential aspects of science instruction.

EL Tips

Review vocabulary with EL students to assure understanding. Ask EL students to describe the intent and focus of the project. Pair EL students with EO (English Only) students when needed. Strongly encourage the journaling aspect of the activities and the use of the Scientific Method and/or the Design Process Reviews.

A Note About Materials

Many materials used in these projects are easy to find and, in most cases, are reusable. Some are school supplies. Virtually all of the materials used in this series are available in local stores—especially wholesale and dollar discount stores. A few are available in local hardware stores. There should always be a sufficient supply of materials for each team.

Refer to individual units for listings of specific materials. Be sure to collect all materials ahead of time, and consider ways to distribute, use, and store materials prior to introducing each new unit. If possible, establish an area in the classroom where materials can be accessed easily.

Addressing Standards

NEXT GENERATION SCIENCE STANDARDS

The National Research Council of the National Academy of Sciences published "A Framework for K–12 Science Education: Practices, Crosscutting Concepts, and Core Ideas." (NRC, 2012)

Its purpose was to serve as a guide for the 26 states presently collaborating to develop the Next Generation Science Standards. The framework defined science "to mean the traditional natural sciences: physics, chemistry, biology, and (more recently) earth, space, and environmental sciences."

The council used the term *engineering* "to mean any engagement in a systematic practice of design to achieve solutions to particular human problems."

They used the term "technology" to include all types of human-made systems and processes—not simply modern computational and communications devices. Technologies result when engineers apply their understanding of the natural world and human behavior to design ways to satisfy human needs and wants.

One of the critical elements of the Next Generation Science Standards is the effort to develop science practices in students. These are the behaviors in which scientists actually engage as they do their investigations. When students or scientists engage in science, they are deeply involved in inquiry as they use a range of skills and knowledge at the same time.

The engineering practices "are the behaviors that engineers engage in as they apply science and math to design solutions to problems." Engineering design has similarities to scientific inquiry. However, there are differences in the two subjects.

Scientific inquiry involves creating a question that can be solved through investigation such as, "What happens when you add alcohol to the liquid?" Try to ask "what" questions instead of "why" questions; they are open-ended and focus on what can be observed during experimentation.

Engineering design involves creating a question that can be solved through design.

"How can I make a boat that moves faster?"

"What happens when I change the dimensions of the boat?"

Engineering questions may produce scientific information. Strengthening the engineering component in these standards helps students recognize the interrelationship between the four cornerstones of STEM instruction: Science, Technology, Engineering, and Math.

The **Disciplinary Core Ideas (DCI)** in the Next Generation Science Standards are broad, essential ideas in science instruction that span across several grade levels and areas of science instruction, including the life sciences, earth and space science, physical sciences, engineering, and technology.

Cross-cutting Concepts are ideas that bridge the boundaries between science and engineering, and help students connect different ideas in the sciences. They provide students with an organizational framework for connecting science and engineering concepts into coherent patterns.

The 7 Cross-cutting Concepts
1. Patterns
2. Cause and Effect
3. Scale, Proportion, and Quantity
4. Systems and System Models
5. Energy and Matter
6. Structure and Function
7. Stability and Change

Most good science activities exhibit examples of several of these concepts, of course, and students should begin to notice these concepts as they do the experiments in this book. Their journals should specify one or more of these concepts each time they write about a project.

Addressing Standards

COMMON CORE STATE STANDARDS

In doing complete, detailed science activities, the math applications are as essential as the apparatus and materials used in the activities. An emphasis on math and reading literacy is built into the Common Core as a prominent aspect of the nearly national consensus that Common Core provides. The application of both skills is essential to STEM education.

Teachers may find that they need to explain the application of a wide variety of math concepts as they arise in STEM activities. These math activities may involve measurement, computing percentages, working with fractions and mixed numbers, measuring and converting units of time, measuring and comparing distances, working with metric units, as well as many others. Students often know the processes in these math concepts but have no idea how to use them in real-life or science applications.

The Common Core State Standards have placed a strong emphasis on math applications, not just the mechanics of a skill. Utilizing math in comparing various results in a science activity will increase understanding of many concepts. Metric measurement—the common system used in science—becomes second nature to students who routinely use it to measure and compare distance, volume, and capacity, for example. Percentages, ratios, and other comparative measurements have more meaning when applied to hands-on activities.

The Common Core Standards are likewise focused on informational reading in science (as well as social studies). Students need to become familiar with sources beyond the textbook in order to research science information. These involve both paper and digital sources.

The writing standards of the Common Core also expect students to routinely write effectively on science topics. The activities in this book provide guided opportunities to take notes and to write brief reports on each activity while including all relevant details.

Common Core State Standards emphasize the development of speaking and listening skills, and they encourage discussion and collaboration. *Stepping into STEM* provides opportunities for students to share their collective writings with each other in The Design Process Review or The Scientific Process Review.

STANDARDS CORRELATIONS

Correlations for both the Common Core State Standards and the Next Generation Science Standards are provided for the units in this book.

General standards correlations for each unit can be found on pages 158–160. You can also visit *www.teachercreated.com/standards* for more comprehensive correlations charts.

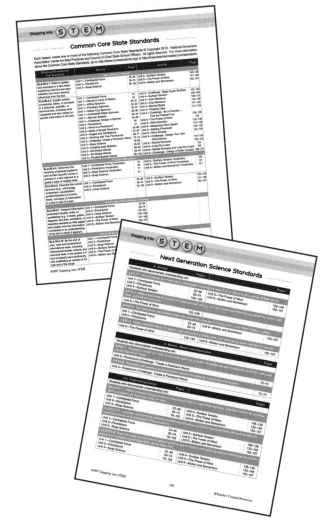

STEM VOCABULARY

The following vocabulary words are used in STEM explorations. Discuss these terms and use them often during the activities and in your journals.

brainstorm—a method of problem solving in which all members of a group spontaneously discuss ideas

collaborate—to work with one or more members in a team to assess the problem or question, determine the nature of the investigation, and analyze results

communicate—to talk with others

data—facts and observations collected to be analyzed

design—an outline or plan

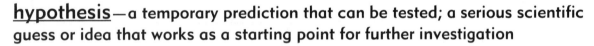

Design Process—a series of steps used by engineers to create products and/or processes

efficient—working well without unusual effort

evaluate—to make a judgment

hypothesis—a temporary prediction that can be tested; a serious scientific guess or idea that works as a starting point for further investigation

inquiry—the process of determining what you wish to learn about a scientific or natural phenomenon

innovation—an improvement of an existing product, system, or way of doing something

invent—the effort to design a solution, modification, or improvement

investigate—the action a scientist takes to learn more about the question

manipulate—to control or change something, often with the hands

modify—to change or adjust

observation—scientific information gathered during an experiment

reaction—a chemical change

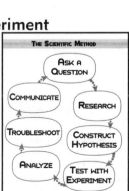

Scientific Method—a series of steps used by scientists to carry out experiments

unique—special or different; unusual; one of a kind

variable—something that can be changed

Teacher Rubric for Assessing Student Performance

STUDENT NAME _____ **DATE** _____

TEAM NAME _____

☐ Pays attention during teacher instruction _____
_____

☐ Follows lesson directions _____
_____

☐ Works well with the team _____
_____

☐ Remains on task during the period _____
_____

☐ Carefully records information, trials, etc. during the investigation _____
_____

☐ Demonstrates creativity in problem solving _____
_____

☐ Demonstrates persistence in problem solving _____
_____

☐ Completes journaling entries _____
_____

☐ Participates in *Design Process Review* _____
_____

COMMENTS: _____
_____
_____

SCORING RUBRIC

4—Excellent Effort and Participation   **2**—Satisfactory Effort and Participation

3—Good Effort and Participation   **1**—Poor or No Effort and Participation

---

TEACHERS: Review the rubrics and the activity pages with students before the activity.

NAME _____ DATE _____

Student Rubric for Assessing Performance

Unit:	Activity:

Directions: Use this rubric to guide you as you work on the activity. Answer the questions by placing an "X" in each box as you go along.

☐ Did I read the project instructions carefully?

☐ Did I discuss the instructions with a partner/team?

☐ Did I set up the materials for the investigation with a partner before beginning?

☐ Did I follow the instructions in the activity carefully and in order?

☐ Did I discuss the progress of the investigation with a partner or the team as we progressed?

☐ Was I prepared to demonstrate the activity with the teacher or class during the period?

☐ Was I prepared to discuss the activity with the teacher or class during the period?

☐ Did I keep records of what happened during the activity?

☐ Did I keep records of engineering designs or changes made?

☐ Did I keep records of results that can be measured in mathematical terms, such as measurements, comparisons, percentages, fractions, and so forth?

☐ Did I record information in the Journal during the journaling activity?

☐ Did I participate in the Design Process Review as a speaker?

COMMENTS: _____

_____

_____

_____

_____

_____

CENTRIPETAL FORCE

6 sessions: 1 session for each activity (approximately 1 to $1\frac{1}{2}$ hours per session)

Focus: Physical Science—Newton's *Laws of Motion*, circular motion, friction, inertia

CONNECTIONS AND SUGGESTIONS

SCIENCE—Students will be exploring centripetal force, a force created by circular motion. Centripetal force pulls or holds rotating objects towards the center of rotation. Students will create a variety of spinners and observe examples of centripetal force including the following:

- A **lifting spinner**, using a small object and circular motion to pull a heavier object toward the center of the motion.

- A **water spinner**, using a cup filled with water pulled toward the center of a moving circle, keeping the water in the cup, even when it briefly goes upside down.

Students will explore the *Laws of Motion* and determine how they relate to the spinners.

They will incorporate appropriate science terminology including *centripetal force, rotating object, circular motion, equilibrium, gravity,* and *laws of motion* into their discussions.

TECHNOLOGY—Students will use computers or tablets to review approved videos and to do additional research on centripetal force and Newton's *Laws of Motion*. Additionally, they may photograph or record their observations and responses as they create a variety of spinners. They will use computers to create charts and, if appropriate, document their observations and experiences.

ENGINEERING—Students will use the design process to create various types of spinners to study centripetal force. They will compare designs for the most efficient spinners in different categories, make improvements, and test and retest designs.

MATH—Math concepts used in this unit include percentages, fractions, ratios, and measurement involving time and distance. Measurement applications will require students to use various methods to measure, by using standard and metric units. Students will be asked to create and share data and to interpret charts, graphs, and spreadsheets.

DISCUSSION PROMPT: Ever wonder why people don't fall out of roller coasters when they go upside down in the loop-de-loop?

A force, known as *centripetal force*, holds people in the cars as long as the roller coaster keeps moving. Engineers who design roller coasters know that centripetal means "center seeking" and use this knowledge when designing coasters. The cars are designed to accelerate when they head into the loop-de-loops that make you go upside down.

As you go around, your *inertia* does two things: it creates an exciting acceleration force and also keeps you in your seat. The power or force you feel is your inertia holding you in the cart against the acceleration trying to pull you away from the coaster floor. The roller coaster track itself keeps the car (and you) from continuing in a straight line and allows it to go up and around.

CENTRIPETAL FORCE

UNIT MATERIALS (for a class of 30 to 35)

- ☐ 100 large plastic or sturdy paper cups
- ☐ 100 regular (not flexi) straws
- ☐ 100 small paper clips
- ☐ 100–500 large paper clips
- ☐ 7 or 8 pounds modeling clay
- ☐ coffee stirrer straws
- ☐ fishing line—8 lb. test or higher (20 lb. test is even easier for students to tie)
- ☐ hole punch

- ☐ math compass or sharp nail
- ☐ rulers—1 per team
- ☐ scissors
- ☐ spring scales or other scales
- ☐ stopwatches or timers
- ☐ tape
- ☐ towels
- ☐ water and pitchers

FIND OUT MORE

A Force Is a Push or a Pull
This short clip explains the term *force* and demonstrates it using balloons.
https://www.youtube.com/watch?v=_LdcxCdB-s8

Centripetal Force (2nd Law of Motion) Planet Nutshell
https://www.youtube.com/watch?v=KvCezk9DJfk

Centripetal Force (Steve Spangler)
https://www.youtube.com/watch?v=yyDRI6iQ9Fw

Isaac Newton
http://www.famousscientists.org/isaac-newton/

NASA Real World Mathematics: Centripetal Force (NASA-eClips video)
This clip offers explanations of centripetal force, inertia, and gravity. You may wish to select the most appropriate sections for student viewing.
https://www.youtube.com/watch?v=PBpe_LLIQJw

Soaring into Science—Force and Motion
https://www.youtube.com/watch?v=xCeaFWlFnk0

TED Talks Newton's Three Laws of Motion
https://www.youtube.com/watch?v=JGO_zDWmkvk

Safety Note: All websites should be checked prior to student viewing to be certain that content is appropriate.

CENTRIPETAL FORCE VOCABULARY

<u>accelerate</u>—move more quickly

<u>base</u>—bottom; the part where something rests or is supported

<u>centripetal force</u>—Centripetal means "center seeking." The force (acting on an object) is constantly following a curved path, seeking the center.

<u>circular</u>—having the form of a circle

<u>equilibrium</u>— a balance between forces

<u>force</u>—a strength or energy that is exerted—a push or a pull
Examples: pushing a door open; a volcano exploding; pushing a button

<u>friction</u>—the action of one surface or object rubbing against another
Examples: sand paper on wood; rubbing hands together to get warm; tires on the road allowing you to accelerate or to stop; striking a match; chewing—teeth on food

<u>gravity</u>—the force that attracts an object toward the center of Earth, or toward any other physical body having mass

<u>inert</u>—not moving

<u>inertia</u>—the tendency of an object at rest to remain at rest and of an object in motion to remain in motion; tendency for an object to keep on doing what it is doing until something forces it to change

<u>mass</u>—a measurement of the amount of matter, or material, that makes up an object, plant, or animal

<u>rotate</u>—to turn around an axis or center
Example: wheel around an axle; Earth rotates around itself every 24 hours

<u>speed</u>—refers to how fast an object is moving (direction is not important, as it is in velocity) *Example:* The car was going 55 mph.

<u>velocity</u>—the measurement of speed in a specific direction
Example: The car was going 55 mph, east.

NAME _____

CENTRIPETAL FORCE

SIR ISAAC NEWTON

Isaac Newton is considered one of the great minds of science. He was born in 1643 in England. He was a physicist, a mathematician, a scientist, and an astronomer.

Newton was a great thinker and had many interests. He used mathematics to explain motion and gravity. His Laws of Motion are still used today to explain the **science of movement.**

It is said that he watched an apple fall from a tree and wondered why it fell down in a straight line. Why didn't it float up in the sky or go sideways? From this question he developed his theory of **gravity**—that mass attracts mass.

Newton's many discoveries about the natural world were very important:

- He improved the telescope.
- He used a prism to show that sunlight is made up of all the colors of the rainbow.
- He discovered that the movement of the tides had to do with gravity and the interaction of the sun, moon, and Earth.
- He helped explain how the planets stay in orbit and how we stay on Earth's surface.
- He decided that the same force of gravity that brought the apple to the ground kept the moon orbiting Earth.
- He discovered **calculus**, the mathematics of change. This discovery allows us to study very small things—like electrons—and very large things—like a galaxy.

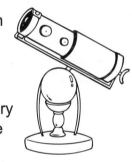

1. Do some research. Write two facts about **gravity**. Note the source of your information.

   Fact 1: _____

   _____

   Fact 2: _____

   _____

   Source: _____

2. Find out more about Newton and his discoveries. Write one more fact.

   Fact 1: _____

   _____

3. Share and discuss your findings with classmates. Create a group poster or chart listing facts or discoveries.

Newton's Laws of Motion

First Law of Motion—The Law of Inertia

Part 1

An object <u>at rest</u> will remain at rest unless acted upon by an outside force.

Example: A ball on the sand will stay where it is until someone kicks it.

Part 2

An object <u>in motion</u> will remain in motion at the same speed and in the same direction unless acted upon by an unbalanced force.

Example: A bike tire will keep turning as the rider pedals until the rider puts on the brakes or the friction of the tire on the road slows the bike down.

Translation for Part 1 and Part 2: *Things want to keep doing what they are doing. They will either stay in motion or at rest.*

Second Law of Motion—Force, Mass, Speed

Force equals mass times acceleration (Force = Mass × Acceleration). The greater the mass of an object, the more force is needed to move it.

Translation: *Force, mass, and speed are related.*

Example: If you push a small child on one swing and push an adult on another swing, it will take more force to get the adult (who has more mass) to move.

Third Law of Motion—Equal and Opposite

For every action, there is an equal and opposite reaction.

Translation: *Every action has a reaction.*

Example: If you blow air into a balloon and then let the balloon go, the air goes in one direction and the balloon goes in the opposite direction.

 NAME _____

LIFTING SPINNERS

Directions: Work in groups of four for this activity exploring centripetal force. Each teammate will gather materials and make a spinner with a different number of large paper clips attached.

1. Fill in the names of each teammate below and see how many paper clips each of you will need to collect.

2. Collect the materials needed to make the spinner.

Teammate 1: _____ 1 small paper clip and 2 large paper clips

Teammate 2: _____ 1 small paper clip and 3 large paper clips

Teammate 3: _____ 1 small paper clip and 4 large paper clips

Teammate 4: _____ 1 small paper clip and 5 large paper clips

> ## TEAM MATERIALS
> - coffee stirrer straws or thin plastic straws
> - fishing line
> - large paper clips
> - rulers
> - small paper clips
> - scissors
> - tape
>
> **TEACHER NOTE:** The straws should have thin openings so that the small paper clips will not slide through them.

PREPARING MATERIALS FOR EACH LIFTING SPINNER

1. Cut a piece of fishing line about 14" to 16" long.

2. If a coffee stirrer is not available, cut a straight piece of plastic straw about 3" or 4" long.

3. Collect the correct number of paper clips for your Lifting Spinner.

MAKING A LIFTING SPINNER

1. Tie one end of the fishing line to a small paper clip. Use two or three knots near the end to keep it tight. (Try not to have a lot of extra line hanging off the knot.)

2. Feed the other end of the fishing line through the stirrer or straw.

3. Tie the correct number of large paper clips to the other end of the fishing line.

4. Use a strip of tape to hold the large paper clips together.

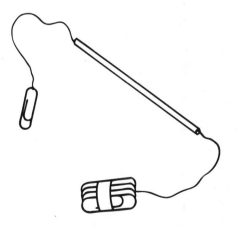

LIFTING SPINNERS

USING THE SPINNER

1. Hold the straw vertically with the small paper clip on top and the appropriate number of large paper clips hanging below.

2. Hold your other hand open, palm up, and rest the large paper clips on it.

3. Use a circular motion to gently rotate the straw. Rotate the straw slowly to get started and then gradually speed up. You should see the small paper clip start to pick up from the straw and move in a circular motion. This will take some practice.

NOTES

✓ You may find that one hand works better than the other to do the circular motion.

✓ Try going in both directions (clockwise or counterclockwise) to see which one works better.

✓ The idea is to get the lighter paper clip to lift up and to start it spinning around. This should pull the large clips off your other hand.

4. Describe what happens to the top and bottom of the spinner when you get it to rotate.

_____

_____

_____

5. Sketch your spinner and how it works here.

 _____

LIFTING SPINNERS

SPINNER OBSERVATIONS

1. Which direction was easier for you to rotate the straw? **CLOCKWISE COUNTERCLOCKWISE**

   Why do you think this was true? _____

   _____

   _____

2. Which hand was easier to use to rotate the straw?   **LEFT   RIGHT**
   Was the hand that worked best your dominant hand (the one you write with)?   **YES NO**

3. Try rotating the straw faster and slower. Which works better?   **FASTER   SLOWER**

   Why do you think this was true? _____

   _____

   _____

4. Was each teammate able to spin his or her lifting spinner? Record the results below.

TEAM	# OF LARGE PAPER CLIPS	ABLE TO SPIN
TEAMMATE 1: _____	2 large paper clips	YES NO
TEAMMATE 2: _____	3 large paper clips	YES NO
TEAMMATE 3: _____	4 large paper clips	YES NO
TEAMMATE 4: _____	5 large paper clips	YES NO

SPINNING VARIATIONS

1. Turn the straw parallel to the ground (horizontal).
   Can you make it work in that direction?   **YES NO**

   Describe your results. _____

   _____

2. Ask a teammate to watch as you try to rotate the
   spinner with your eyes closed. Can you do it?   **YES NO**

   Explain. _____

   _____

NAME _____

LIFTING SPINNERS

ADDING MORE WEIGHT TO THE SPINNERS

Directions: Continue working in groups of four for this activity. Each teammate will gather materials and make a spinner with more large paper clips attached than during the first session.

1. Fill in the names of each teammate below and see how many paper clips each of you will need to collect.

2. Collect the materials needed to make the new spinner.

   Teammate 1: _Levi_____ 1 small paper clip and 6 large paper clips

   Teammate 2: _Anthony + Chloe + Amy_ 1 small paper clip and 7 large paper clips

   Teammate 3: _Alex_____ 1 small paper clip and 8 large paper clips

   Teammate 4: _Jack Adyn_____ 1 small paper clip and 9 large paper clips

3. Use the same materials used in the first activity in order to create new lifting spinners.

4. Add the correct number of large paper clips to the fishing line and tape the paper clips together (loosely).

5. Take turns testing each new spinner. Start with the one with 6 large paper clips.

6. Was each teammate able to spin his or her lifting spinner? Record the results below.

TEAM	# OF LARGE PAPER CLIPS	ABLE TO SPIN
TEAMMATE 1: _____	6 large paper clips	YES NO
TEAMMATE 2: _____	7 large paper clips	YES NO
TEAMMATE 3: _____	8 large paper clips	YES NO
TEAMMATE 4: _____	9 large paper clips	YES NO

7. What was the highest number of large paper clips you lifted with just one small paper clip?

8. Could you add more paper clips?   **YES**   **NO**   Do so if time allows.

9. Discuss your results.

_____

_____

_____

N A M E

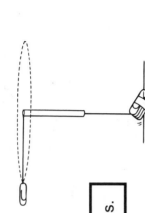

LIFTING SPINNERS

DO THE MATH!

Directions: Compute the weight ratios below. The first two have been done for you.

| KEY | A small paper clip weighs about 1 gram.   A large paper clip weighs about 2 grams. |

RATIOS

1 small paper clip to 1 large paper clip is 1 gram to 2 grams or a ratio of 1 to 2—written $\frac{1}{2}$ or 1:2 (one to two)

1 small paper clip to 2 large paper clips is 1 gram to 4 grams or a ratio of 1 to 4—written $\frac{1}{4}$ or 1:4 (one to four)

1 small paper clip to 3 large paper clips is 1 gram to _____ grams or a ratio of 1 to _____ written $\frac{1}{\Box}$ or 1:$\Box$

1 small paper clip to 4 large paper clips is 1 gram to _____ grams or a ratio of 1 to _____ written $\frac{1}{\Box}$ or 1:$\Box$

1 small paper clip to 5 large paper clips is 1 gram to _____ grams or a ratio of 1 to _____ written $\frac{1}{\Box}$ or 1:$\Box$

1 small paper clip to 6 large paper clips is 1 gram to _____ grams or a ratio of 1 to _____ written $\frac{1}{\Box}$ or 1:$\Box$

1 small paper clip to 7 large paper clips is 1 gram to _____ grams or a ratio of 1 to _____ written $\frac{1}{\Box}$ or 1:$\Box$

LIFTING SPINNERS

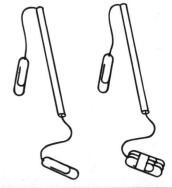

VARIATION 1—LARGE CLIP ON TOP

1. Each teammate should replace the small paper clip on one of his or her spinners with a large paper clip. Try to use spinners with different numbers of large paper clips on the bottom.

2. Write your name and number of clips in the chart below.

3. Retest the spinners.

4. Name your team and record each teammate's results.

TEAM: _____	# OF LARGE PAPER CLIPS ON THE BOTTOM	RESULTS
TEAMMATE 1: _____	_____	_____
TEAMMATE 2: _____	_____	_____
TEAMMATE 3: _____	_____	_____
TEAMMATE 4: _____	_____	_____

VARIATION 2—LONGER FISHING LINE

1. Each teammate should create a spinner with 24" of fishing line. Use a large paper clip on the top and a different number of clips on the bottom.

2. Test the spinners again.

3. Remember to rest the paper clips (on the bottom) in one hand and let them lift off as you spin with the other hand.

4 What happens? Record the results.

24" LIFTING SPINNER	# OF LARGE CLIPS ON THE BOTTOM	RESULTS
TEAMMATE 1: _____		
TEAMMATE 2: _____		
TEAMMATE 3: _____		
TEAMMATE 4: _____		

LIFTING SPINNERS

JOURNAL ENTRY

1. How did you get the paper clips to lift off your hand? _____

_____

_____

2. Describe your technique to keep the spinner spinning? _____

_____

_____

3. Did it make a difference whether you held the straw horizontally or vertically? **YES   NO**

   If yes, which way worked better?   **HORIZONTAL   VERTICAL**

   Explain. _____

   _____

4. What difference did doubling the length of the fishing line make?

_____

_____

_____

5. Would this type of spinner make a good toy? Why or why not?

_____

_____

_____

6. What surprised you the most about lifting spinners?

_____

_____

_____

DESIGN PROCESS REVIEW—LIFTING SPINNERS

Directions: Gather with your teacher and class. Use this journal entry and your other documentation about your experiences with Lifting Spinners. Take turns sharing your observations about centripetal force.

PLANETARY SPINNERS

Directions: Work in small groups to make your own spinners. You will need 1 piece of fishing line about 12" long, 2 small paper clips, a plastic straw, and 1-ounce of modeling clay to make a personal Planetary Spinner.

TEAM MATERIALS

- fishing line
- spring scale or other measuring scale
- modeling clay
- plastic straws (straight, not flexi)
- rulers
- scissors
- small paper clips

NOTE: Modeling clay is easily sliced into 1-ounce segments with dental floss or a table knife.

PREPARING MATERIALS FOR THE PLANETARY SPINNER

1. Cut a piece of fishing line about 12" to 14" long.
2. Cut a straight piece of plastic straw about 4" long.

MAKING A PLANETARY SPINNER

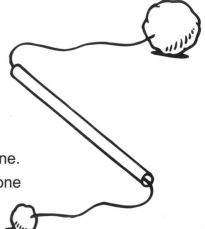

1. Tie one end of the fishing line to a small paper clip.
2. Feed the other end of the fishing line through the straw.
3. Tie the other small paper clip to the other end of the fishing line.
4. Cut about $\frac{1}{4}$ of the 1 ounce of clay and wrap it firmly around one of the paper clips. This clay ball will represent the moon.
5. Form a ball around the other paper clip with the remaining $\frac{3}{4}$ ounce of clay. This ball will represent Earth.

USING THE SPINNER

1. Hold the straw or stirrer vertically in one hand. The moon should be on top.
2. Place the other hand under the straw and gently hold the Earth. The fishing line will be loose under the straw.
3. Gently rotate the straw in a circular motion to start. Gradually pick up speed. The smaller ball of clay—the moon—should begin to spin around.
4. As the "moon" spins, it should pick up Earth, the larger ball of clay. You should be able to drop the hand that was holding Earth and keep spinning.
5. Sketch your Planetary Spinner in motion.

PLANETARY SPINNERS

HOW DOES IT WORK?

The rotating movement and the weight of the small clay ball (moon) combine to exert force on the heavier ball of clay (Earth) and lift it. The spinner shows that the lighter clay object can lift the heavier clay object with the power of centripetal force.

Directions: Continue to work in small groups for this activity using your Planetary Spinners. You will need scales for this measurement activity.

PLANETARY SPINNER—ADJUSTING THE WEIGHT

1. Weigh the moon and the Earth and record the weights in grams or ounces on the chart below. (Trial 1)

2. Remove a small amount of clay from the moon and add it to the larger clay ball, Earth.

3. Add the new weights to the chart.

4. Retest the spinner. (Trial 2)

5. Did changing the weight of the Earth and moon by adjusting the amount of clay affect the way the spinner works?   **YES   NO**

   Explain. _____

   _____

6. Gradually make the clay moon smaller and the clay Earth larger. Do two more trials. See how small (and light) you can make the moon and still have it be able to lift Earth.

7. Continue recording the adjusted weights for each of your spinner tests on the chart below.

8. Figure out how much heavier the Earth model was than the moon model in each trial. Record the differences in the fourth column of the chart.

	WEIGHT OF MOON (ounce or gram)	WEIGHT OF EARTH (ounce or gram)	DIFFERENCE
TRIAL 1			
TRIAL 2			
TRIAL 3			
TRIAL 4			

PLANETARY SPINNERS

JOURNAL ENTRY

1. Was the Planetary Spinner easier or more difficult to work than the Lifting Spinner?

   Explain. _____

   _____

   _____

   _____

2. Was it easier to spin the planetary spinner when the moon was *larger* or *smaller*?

   Explain. _____

   _____

   _____

   _____

3. Explain the science idea you learned in doing this activity. _____

   _____

   _____

   _____

4. Would a Planetary Spinner make a good toy? Why or why not? _____

   _____

   _____

   _____

5. What surprised you the most about Planetary Spinners? _____

   _____

   _____

   _____

DESIGN PROCESS REVIEW—PLANETARY SPINNERS

Directions: Gather with your teacher and class. Take turns sharing your observations, journal entries, and other documentation about your experiences with Planetary Spinners. How can you relate them to Newton's Laws?

WATER-CUP SPINNERS

TEACHER PREPARATION: This activity should be done outdoors, and everyone should expect to get wet. Adult supervision should be provided to help students poke holes in the cups.

> **TEAM MATERIALS**
> - fishing line
> - hole punch, math compass, or sharp nail
> - plastic straws (straight)
> - rulers
> - scissors
> - sturdy paper cups
> - towels
> - water and pitchers

PREPARING THE WATER-CUP SPINNER

1. Make two holes near the top of a sturdy cup. The holes should be on opposite sides of the cup just below the rim.
2. Cut 18"–24" of fishing line and tie one end to one hole in the cup. Make about three knots to keep it tight.
3. Cut the plastic straw in half to make a handle. You will need a 3"–4" section. It should fit across the palm of your hand.
4. Feed the fishing line through the straw.
5. Tie the other end of the fishing line to the other hole in the cup. Again, try to make three knots.
6. This cup will be a *centripetal force generator*. Test it by pulling the cup and the handle to make certain the fishing line is secure on both sides.

TESTING THE CUP SPINNER—TRIAL 1

1. Gather towels and the spinners and go outside. Allow enough room to spin the spinners out to the side without interfering with other students' tests.
2. Fill the cup half full of water. Lift the cup of water by the straw "handle."
3. Gently swing the cup in a circle. Start with the cup by your feet and swing it up—over your head. Gradually increase the speed of your swing.

> **Tip:** If it is hard to hold the cup or if the straw bends too much, ask an adult to slit the other half of the straw you used lengthwise. Wrap the slit straw over the straw handle and tape it on. This will make the handle twice as strong.

4. What happens to the water in the cup when you swing the cup around?

   Does water spill out?

   ### YES NO

   If yes, how much?

   ### SOME   MOST   ALL

5. Draw how much water was in the cup *before* and *after* spinning.

BEFORE | AFTER

WATER-CUP SPINNERS

Directions: Use the water-cup spinner you made in Trial 1.

TESTING THE CUP SPINNER—TRIAL 2

1. Fill the cup $\frac{3}{4}$ full of water.
2. Gently swing the cup in a circle again. Gradually increase the speed of your swing.
3. What happened to the water in the cup this time? Did water spill?

   YES   NO

   If yes, how much?

   SOME   MOST   ALL

4. Draw how much water was in the cup before and after spinning.

BEFORE   AFTER

TESTING THE CUP SPINNER—TRIAL 3

1. Fill the cup with water almost to the top. Leave about 1 centimeter from the rim of the cup.
2. Gently swing the cup in a circle again. Gradually increase the speed of your swing.
3. What happened to the water in the cup this time? Did water spill?

   YES   NO

   If yes, how much?

   SOME   MOST   ALL

4. Draw how much water was in the cup before and after spinning.

BEFORE   AFTER

Extension: What happens if you try to spin around (your whole body) so that the fishing line and cup are parallel to the ground?

Did water spill?   **YES   NO**   If yes, how much?   **SOME   MOST   ALL**

★ ★ ★ SAVE THE CUP SPINNER FOR THE NEXT ACTIVITY ★ ★ ★

WATER-CUP SPINNERS

JOURNAL ENTRY

1. What surprised you the most about using Cup Spinners? _____

_____

_____

_____

2. What was the most difficult part of working the Cup Spinners? _____

_____

_____

_____

3. Explain why teamwork was important in this activity. _____

_____

_____

_____

4. Explain how this activity relates to Newton's Laws of Motion. _____

_____

_____

_____

_____

_____

5. Why do you think the cup acts as a centripetal force generator? _____

_____

_____

_____

DESIGN PROCESS REVIEW—WATER CUP SPINNERS

Directions: Gather with your teacher and class. Take turns sharing your observations, journal entries, and other documentation about your experiences with Cup Spinners.

CENTRIPETAL WATER SPINNERS

Directions: Work in pairs. Use the Cup Spinners you constructed in the last activity. This activity should also be done outside, and you should expect to get wet. Take turns testing each other's spinners.

> **TEAM MATERIALS**
> - Cup Spinners from Activity 3
> - math compass or sharp nail
> - towels
> - water and pitchers or extra cups

MAKING A CENTRIPETAL WATER SPINNER

1. Use the Cup Spinner from the previous activity. It should be empty.
2. With adult supervision, use a math compass or a sharp nail to poke four evenly-spaced holes in the cup. The holes should be about $\frac{1}{4}$ to $\frac{1}{2}$ inch above the base of the cups.
3. Gather towels and the spinners and go outside.
4. Find an area that will allow enough room to spin the spinners without interfering with other students' tests.

TESTING A CENTRIPETAL WATER SPINNER

1. **Teammate 1** will hold his or her spinner handle while **Teammate 2** twists the cup so that the fishing line twists into a tight line.
2. Then, **Teammate 1** will hold the cup *and* the straw handle while **Teammate 2** gets another paper cup of the same size and slips it over the cup with the holes.
3. While **Teammate 1** holds the cup and the handle, **Teammate 2** will fill the inner cup with water and put the water pitcher down.
4. When both team members are ready, **Teammate 2** will quickly pull off the outside cup and jump back.

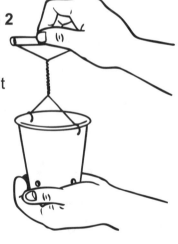

CENTRIPETAL WATER SPINNER OBSERVATIONS

1. Watch the cup as the water drains out of the holes in the bottom. Describe what happens.

   _____

   _____

   _____

   _____

2. In the frame, draw the way the water flows out of the cup.

CENTRIPETAL WATER SPINNERS

JOURNAL ENTRY

1. What forces acted on the water and the cup? _____

_____

_____

_____

2. What was the most difficult part of the test? _____

_____

_____

_____

3. Did the water flow the way you expected it to flow out of the cup?   **YES   NO**

   Explain. _____

_____

_____

4. Compare your team's results with your observations of other teams' experiences.

_____

_____

_____

_____

5. Brainstorm a list of toys or tools you could make using what you learned today?

_____

_____

_____

DESIGN PROCESS REVIEW—CENTRIPETAL WATER SPINNERS

Directions: Gather with your teacher and class. Take turns sharing your observations, journal entries, and other documentation about your experiences with Centripetal Water Spinners.

SPINNER SPEEDS

Directions: Each pair of students will make two new centripetal water spinners. One spinner will have four holes and the other will have eight smaller holes. Teammates will take turns testing and timing each other's water spinners to see which version spins and empties faster. This activity should be done outside. Getting wet is likely.

> ## TEAM MATERIALS
> - fishing line
> - hole punch
> - math compass or sharp nail
> - plastic straws or stirrers (straight)
> - scissors
> - sturdy paper cups
> - towels
> - stopwatches or timers
> - water

Directions: Before testing, take a poll and tally which cup each student thinks will empty faster.

	TALLY MARKS	TOTALS
8 Small Holes		
4 Larger Holes		

4-HOLE AND 8-HOLE CENTRIPETAL WATER SPINNERS

1. Make a water spinner with 8 small holes (●) and another with 4 larger holes ⬤. The holes should be about $\frac{1}{2}$ inch above the bottom of the cup.

2. Decide which teammate will test each cup.

3. Cover each completed spinner cup with another cup of the same size—but no holes.

4. Place the cup spinners on a flat surface. Try not to tangle the handles.

TEST PREPARATION

1. Choose a water spinner to test and have water and a timer ready.

2. Decide with your partner how to time the spinner once the second cup has been pulled off. The goal is to see how many seconds it takes for the water to empty out of the spinner cup. Check the option below that you plan to use, or describe your alternative plan.

☐ **Option 1:** The partner holding the handle also holds the timer while the other partner pulls the cup.

☐ **Option 2:** The partner pulling the cup also tries to start the timer.

☐ **Option 3:** _____

(N)(A)(M)(E) _____

SPINNER SPEEDS

READY, SET, GO!

1. Spread out and prepare to test your 4-hole and 8-hole spinners.

2. When a teacher or other observer calls "**START**," pull off the outer cup and start timing.

3. Count the seconds until the cup is empty and has stopped spinning.

4. Jot down the time for each test. You will need to add this information to a chart at the end of the activity.

5. Switch positions and time your partner's spinning cup. Record the results on the chart (see pages 42–43).

SPINNER SPEEDS

Directions: Use a computer to make a chart like the one on page 43 to compare the recorded times gathered after using water spinners that have eight small holes to water spinners that have four large holes.

CHARTING RESULTS—TECHNOLOGY PROCEDURES

1. Open **Word**® or **Google Docs**™.

2. Click on the **Table** and insert a table. You will need to fill in how many rows and columns you need.

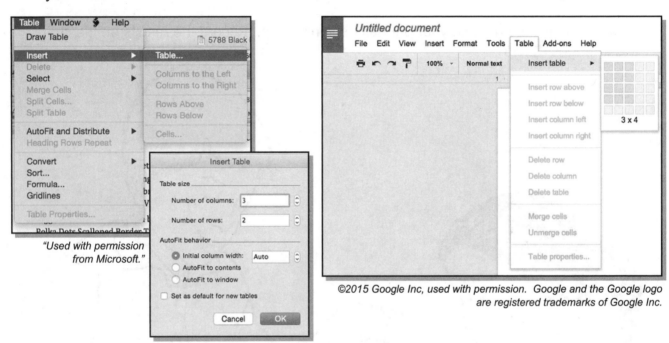

"Used with permission from Microsoft."

©2015 Google Inc, used with permission. Google and the Google logo are registered trademarks of Google Inc.

3. The chart should have 3 columns. You will need to decide how many rows to include. You should have a row for each student who is participating.

4. Your empty chart will appear on your page.

5. You can make adjustments by going back to **Table** on the menu bar. You can make the size of the cells different and you can add or delete rows and columns.

6. Label the chart and fill in the students' names and the times.

SPINNER SPEEDS

Directions: Use this chart for note-taking or for your data display if a computer is unavailable.

SPINNER SPEEDS		
STUDENT NAMES	4 LARGE HOLES	8 SMALL HOLES

NAME _____

SPINNER SPEEDS

JOURNAL ENTRY

1. Describe what you learned from today's activity. _____

   _____

   _____

   _____

   _____

2. How can you increase the speed of a centripetal spinner? _____

   _____

   _____

   _____

3. What special problems did you and your partner face doing this activity? _____

   _____

   _____

   _____

4. How did you resolve the problems you faced? _____

   _____

   _____

   _____

5. What did you learn about centripetal force that might be useful to a gardener or someone who takes care of plants?

   _____

   _____

   _____

DESIGN PROCESS REVIEW—SPINNER SPEEDS

Directions: Gather with your teacher and class. Take turns sharing your observations, journal entries, and other documentation about your experiences with spinner speeds. Don't forget to explain how Newton's Laws factor in!

 NAME _____

CHALLENGE: DESIGN A SPINNER

Directions: Make a spinner of your own design. Try to make one that could be used as a real tool or toy. Plan on using materials from activities in the unit and other, teacher-approved materials from the classroom or recycling area.

BRAINSTORM: Think about what you have learned about the Laws of Motion and centripetal force. Was there a spinner you wished you could do again but with an adjustment? Is there a different type of spinner you might like to try? Now is your chance!

What would you like to make for this challenge and why? _____

_____

_____

Will you need to do extra research?   **YES   NO**

If yes, what do you want to find out? _____

_____

_____

DESIGN THE SOLUTION: Sketch your plan here. Add notes as needed.

_____

_____

_____

_____

_____

_____

_____

_____

_____

BUILD: Construct your spinner using materials from Activities 1–5. Use additional materials if approved by your teacher.

List the materials you will be using below. If you need more room, use the back of this page.

_____ _____ _____

_____ _____ _____

CHALLENGE: DESIGN A SPINNER

EVALUATE: What was the most interesting part of the construction process? _____

_____

_____

_____

Did your design work as you planned? **YES   NO**

Explain: _____

_____

_____

MODIFY: What adjustments can you make to improve your spinner? List them and sketch your plan below. Then make the adjustments and retest your spinner.

ADJUSTMENTS: _____

_____

SHARE: Describe the results of your project. _____

_____

_____

Explain what your spinner might be used to do in a real-world setting. _____

_____

_____

_____

 **2**

PENDULUMS

4 sessions: 1 session for each activity (approximately 1 to $1\frac{1}{2}$ hours per session)

Focus: Physical Science—the nature and behavior of pendulums, Newton's Laws of Motion, friction, inertia

CONNECTIONS AND SUGGESTIONS

SCIENCE—Students will be working with pendulums. They will learn about Galileo's early studies of pendulums and will work in teams to create a variety of pendulums that have different lengths and weights. They will review Newton's Laws of Motion and how they relate to pendulums.

They will also discover that when two pendulums transfer energy back and forth between each other, one will slow down as the other speeds up. This is called the *transfer of energy*.

TECHNOLOGY—Students may use computers or tablets to review approved videos and to do additional research on pendulums, Galileo, and Newton and his Laws of Motion. Additionally, they may photograph or record their observations and responses as they create a variety of pendulums. They may use computers to create charts and document their observations and experiences.

ENGINEERING—Students will build a variety of pendulums and observe their motions. They will experiment with different types of bobs and different pendulum lengths. They will compare the pendulums, make improvements, test, and retest.

MATH—Math concepts used in this unit include measurement in length (inches and feet). Students will also measure time. They will calculate the duration of the pendulum's swing and the period of a swing. Students will be asked to share data and to create and interpret charts, graphs, and spreadsheets.

DISCUSSION PROMPT: Let's talk about pendulums.

A grandfather clock has a pendulum that swings back and forth to keep the time. A metronome is a pendulum used to keep time in music. It can be adjusted to move slowly or rapidly. A playground swing is another type of pendulum. It hangs from a cross bar or pivot. To get a swing moving back and forth, you need to start pumping or to get a push.

Gradually, a swing slows if you do not keep pushing it or pumping. Each time it moves forward or back, it goes a shorter distance. Have you ever wondered why one push couldn't keep you going forever? It is the air! The air pushes against you in the swing and causes friction. The friction is what slows the swing, or pendulum, down.

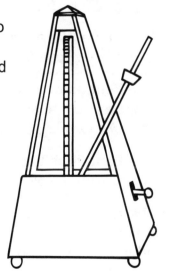

PENDULUMS

UNIT MATERIALS (for a class of 30 to 35)

- ☐ 1-minute timers or stopwatches
- ☐ 200–500 large paper clips, 100 large metal washers, or 100 large metal nuts
- ☐ 36" rod (rounded dowels, bamboo stakes, PVC pipe, or broom sticks)
- ☐ fishing line—8 pound test or higher (20 lb. test is even easier for students to tie)
- ☐ masking tape or duct tape
- ☐ protractors
- ☐ rulers
- ☐ dial spring scales (grams)
- ☐ spring scales

NOTES

_____

_____

_____

_____

_____

_____

_____

_____

_____

_____

_____

_____

FIND OUT MORE

Pendulum Wave Demonstration
https://www.youtube.com/watch?v=YhMiuzyU1ag

The Pendulum and Galileo—ways to challenge and test knowledge; three important properties of the pendulum
https://www.youtube.com/watch?v=MpzaCCbX-z4

The Pendulum Wave Machine
http://www.eepybird.com/experiments/pendulumwave/

The Spangler Effect - Newton's Pendulum Season 01 Episode 04
https://www.youtube.com/watch?v=0lhuyUJbuNc

Safety Note: All websites should be checked prior to student viewing to be certain that content is appropriate.

NAME _____

PENDULUMS VOCABULARY

<u>arc</u>—something arched or curved; a curved path (*Example:* a rainbow forms an arc.) ⌢

<u>bob</u>—the weight—usually wood or metal—attached to the string or wire to create a pendulum

<u>fixed support</u>—the frame the pendulum is attached to at the pivot

<u>inert</u>—at rest; not moving (*Example:* When a pendulum is hanging down and is still, it is inert.)

<u>force</u>—a strength or energy that is exerted; a push or a pull

<u>friction</u>—the action of one surface or object rubbing against another. Friction gradually will slow an object in motion. (*Example:* A swing will eventually slow down due to friction. In this case the "surface" being rubbed is the air.)

<u>gravity</u>—the force that pulls one object towards another

<u>oscillation</u>—one complete back and forth movement

<u>pendulum</u>—a weight (bob) suspended from a fixed point (pivot) that can swing freely

<u>period</u>—the interval of time it takes (a pendulum) to swing from **A** to **B** and back again; the period of a swing depends on the length of the wire (fishing line) and the force of gravity, not the weight of the bob

<u>perpendicular</u>—forming right angles (90°)

<u>parallel</u>—always the same distance apart; extending in the same direction

<u>pivot</u>—the point where the string or wire is attached to the rod

<u>simultaneously</u>—at the same time

<u>taut</u>—tight, with no slack in the line

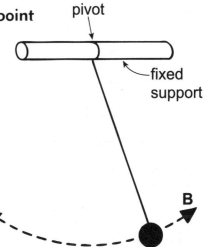

PENDULUMS

WHO KNEW?

SWINGING CHANDELIER

GALILEO GALILEI

A long time ago, Galileo said that science required proof. He did a lot of the research on the pendulum. His research started in a great church in Pisa, Italy. Galileo wasn't paying attention in the church. At least, he wasn't paying attention to the priest.

The swaying back and forth of the hanging lights distracted him. They had a rhythm. He wondered how they kept moving. How was force being applied to make them move?

He was a good scientist and he went home and experimented. He made different models. He observed the movements. This helped him understand the pendulum better.

He believed that experiments were a good way to prove his ideas. He also believed that other scientists should be able to test his work.

1. Do some research. Find out more about Galileo's life and interests. Write three facts.

   Fact 1: _____

   _____

   Fact 2: _____

   _____

   Fact 3: _____

   _____

2. Continue researching. List 3 discoveries Galileo is known for and describe what each does.

   Discovery 1: _____

   _____

   Discovery 2: _____

   _____

   Discovery 3: _____

   _____

3. Share and discuss your findings with classmates.

4. Create a group poster or other display about Galileo Galilei.

WHAT IS A PENDULUM?

Anything that swings from its own weight can be called a **pendulum**. A tire swing is a good example. A grandfather's clock usually has a pendulum—a weight on a long rod. These are called "simple" pendulums because they only swing back and forth.

A pendulum is made of two parts. The first part is a rope, wire, or string that hangs from a fixed support (rod). The fixed support does not move. This wire has a weight at the bottom. The second part, the **bob**, is the weight.

A pendulum will continue to swing for a long time. *Gravity* is the force that pulls the weight. *Friction* from the air will gradually slow the movement of the weight.

The time it takes a bob to complete a cycle moving forward and back is called the **period**. This cycle is called an **oscillation**.

The longer the string or wire, the longer the period will be.

1. Do some research. What are some everyday examples of pendulums?

   _____

   _____

   _____

2. Draw and label an example of a pendulum in motion. Label its parts. Use arrows to show the movement. Explain what the pendulum does.

 _____

MAKE A SIMPLE PENDULUM

Directions: Work in pairs to make a pendulum.

TEAM MATERIALS
- 36" rods
- fishing line
- large paper clips
- masking tape or duct tape

- protractors (see page 55 for template)
- rulers
- scales (grams)
- stopwatches or 1-minute timers

MAKING A SIMPLE PENDULUM

1. Place a rod so that it connects two desks or tables. There should be a foot or more of free space between the two pieces of furniture. Tape the rod down on each end to secure it.

   How many inches are in 3 feet? _____   How many feet are in 1 yard? _____

2. Tape four paper clips together to form a bob. (A large paper clip weighs about 2 grams.)

   Explain what a **bob** is in your own words. _____

   _____

   Weigh the bob. How much does it weigh? _____ **grams**

3. Cut a 15" piece of fishing line. Tie one end of the fishing line to the middle of the rod. This will be your **pivot point**.

4. Tie the other end of the fishing line to the bob. Adjust the length so that the pendulum is 12" long from the rod to the bob. Roll the stick or retie the line to get the pendulum the correct length.

5. When the bob hangs straight down it is inert. It should form a 90° angle from the rod.

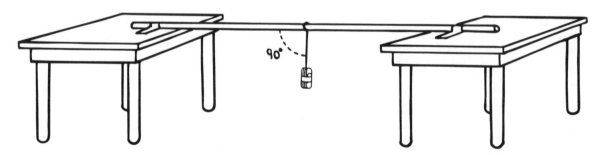

6. Choose the correct vocabulary words to complete the following sentences.

   > perpendicular   parallel

   The bob is _____ to the floor when it is held at a 90° angle from its starting position.

   When the bob is *inert*, it hangs down and is _____ to the ground.

 **NAME** _____

MAKE A SIMPLE PENDULUM

Directions: Read through ALL the directions for the activity before you begin. The pendulum activities in this unit require a stopwatch or timer and a protractor. Be aware of your responsibilities and your partner's responsibilities.

TESTING A SIMPLE 12" PENDULUM

1. Look at a protractor. Find 90°. Make sure the rod and the pendulum create a 90° angle.

2. Hold the bob parallel to the floor. Keep the line taut. Let the bob go!

3. Observe the swing of the pendulum. Does it swing freely?   **YES   NO**

   Does it swing higher or lower than the rod?   **HIGHER   LOWER   EQUAL**

4. Stop the pendulum. Make any needed adjustments to help it swing freely.

5. Complete the *Find the Angles* worksheet on page 54.

TIMING AN OSCILLATION

1. What is an **oscillation**? Explain it in your own words. _____

   _____

   _____

2. The time for one complete oscillation is called the **period**. You can time the period using a stopwatch or a classroom clock with a second hand.

3. **Partner 1:** Hold the pendulum at a 90° angle. The line should be taut and parallel to the floor.

   Partner 2: Get ready to time the oscillation.

   Partner 1: Let the pendulum go back and forth once. Yell **STOP** when it comes back to you.

   Partner 2: Stop the timer and record the time below.

   It took _____ seconds for one complete oscillation.

   The **period** is _____ seconds.

4. Switch roles and time the oscillation again. Add your data below.

   It took _____ seconds for one complete oscillation.

   The **period** is _____ seconds.

5. Sketch the **period** in the frame. Use arrows to show direction.

★ ★ ★ SAVE THE PENDULUMS FOR ACTIVITY 2 ★ ★ ★

MAKE A SIMPLE PENDULUM

FIND THE ANGLES

Directions: Mark the following angles on the protractors below. Use this sheet for reference when working with pendulums.

30°

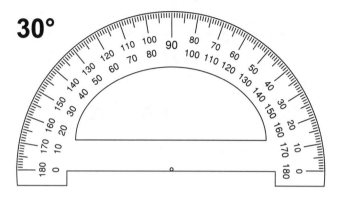

45°

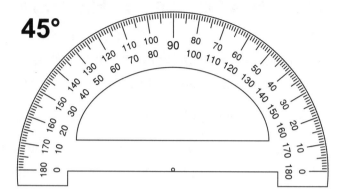

60°

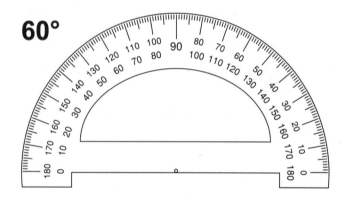

90°

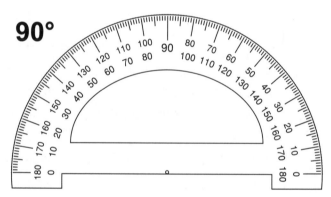

135°

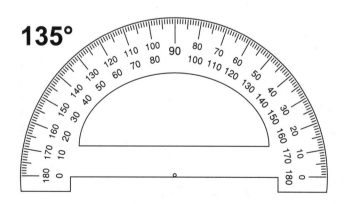

180°

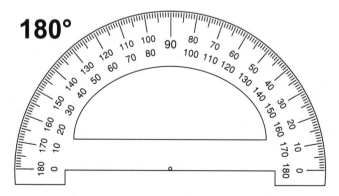

MAKE A SIMPLE PENDULUM

PROTRACTOR

Directions: Make copies of the protractor on heavy paper for each team. Laminate them if possible. Protractors can also be slid onto the rods to help students find the angles. Cut a hole the appropriate size and add the protractor to the rod (fixed support).

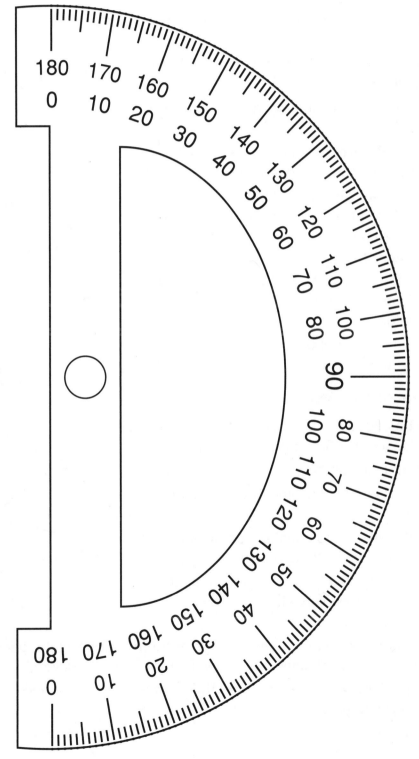

MAKE A SIMPLE PENDULUM

12" PENDULUM—DIFFERENT ANGLES

Directions: Read through ALL the directions for the activity before you begin. Work in pairs.
Use the 12" pendulum for this activity. You will be varying the degrees of the angles.

OSCILLATIONS AT 90 DEGREES

1. Work with a partner to count the number of oscillations
   for a one-minute period.

2. **Partner 1:** Hold the 12" pendulum at a 90° angle
   (from the floor).

   Partner 2: Get ready to time the pendulum's
   movements.

3. **Partner 1:** Prepare to count the oscillations while
   your partner is timing the pendulum.

   Partner 2: Say "**GO**," and start the timer. Keep
   timing until the pendulum stops moving or you hit
   the 1-minute mark.

4. Do four trials. Each partner will have two turns
   releasing the pendulum at a 90° angle and counting
   the oscillations and two turns timing the pendulum
   for 1 minute.

5. Record the number of oscillations on the chart on page 58
   or make your own chart using the directions on page 59.

Get ready!

OSCILLATIONS AT 60 DEGREES

1. You will be counting the oscillations of the pendulum
   when released at a 60° angle.

2. **Partner 1:** Hold the 12" pendulum at a 60° angle.

   Partner 2: Get ready to time the pendulum's
   movements.

3. **Partner 1:** Prepare to count the oscillations while
   your partner is timing the pendulum.

   Partner 2: Say "**GO**," and start the timer. Keep
   timing until the pendulum stops moving or you hit
   the 1-minute mark.

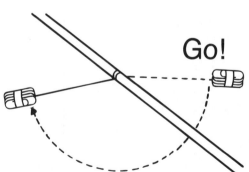

Go!

4. Do four trials. Each partner should have two turns releasing the pendulum at a 60° angle
   and counting the oscillations and two turns timing the pendulum.

5. Record the number of oscillations on the chart on page 58 or make your own chart using
   the directions on page 59.

 **NAME** _____

MAKE A SIMPLE PENDULUM

6" PENDULUM—DIFFERENT ANGLES

Directions: Read through ALL the directions for the activity before you begin. Work in pairs. You will be changing the length of the pendulum line to 6" in these activities.

OSCILLATIONS AT 90 DEGREES

1. Shorten the length of the fishing line by half. To do this, wrap the line around the rod at the top until it is 6 inches long. (See the diagram below on the right.) You don't need to untie the pendulum.

2. Tape the fishing line to the rod.

3. Test the 6" pendulum at its new length.

   Partner 1: Hold the 6" pendulum at a 90° angle.

   Partner 2: Get ready to time the pendulum's movements.

4. **Partner 1:** Prepare to count the oscillations while your partner is timing the pendulum for 1 minute.

   Partner 2: Say "**GO**," and start the timer. Keep timing until the pendulum stops moving or you hit the 1-minute mark.

5. Do four trials. Each partner should have two turns releasing the pendulum at a 90° angle and counting the oscillations and two turns timing the pendulum for 1 minute.

6. Record the number of oscillations on the chart that is on page 58 or make your own chart using the directions on page 59.

OSCILLATIONS AT 60 DEGREES

1. Use your 6" pendulum again. This time you will adjust the angle. Mark the 60° on the protractor on the right.

2. Test the pendulum at a 60° angle.

   Partner 1: Hold the 6" pendulum at a 60° angle.

   Partner 2: Get ready to time the pendulum's movements.

3. **Partner 1:** Prepare to count the oscillations while your partner is timing the pendulum for 1 minute.

   Partner 2: Say "**GO**," and start the timer. Keep timing until the pendulum stops moving or until you hit the 1-minute mark.

4. Do four trials. Each partner should have two turns releasing the pendulum at a 60° angle and counting the oscillations and two turns timing the pendulum for 1 minute.

5. Record the number of oscillations on the chart on page 58 or make your own chart using the directions on page 59.

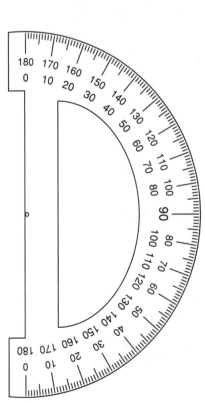

N A M E _____

MAKE A SIMPLE PENDULUM

12" PENDULUM OSCILLATIONS—1 MINUTE

TRIAL	TRIAL 1	TRIAL 2	TRIAL 3	TRIAL 4
NAME				
90°				
60°				

6" PENDULUM OSCILLATIONS—1 MINUTE

TRIAL	TRIAL 1	TRIAL 2	TRIAL 3	TRIAL 4
NAME				
90°				
60°				

MAKE A SIMPLE PENDULUM

CHARTING RESULTS—TECHNOLOGY PROCEDURE

Use a computer to make a chart to compare the oscillations of the 12" long pendulum and the 6" long pendulum.

1. Open **Word** or **Google Docs**.

2. Click on the **Table** and insert a table. You will need to fill in how many rows and columns you need.

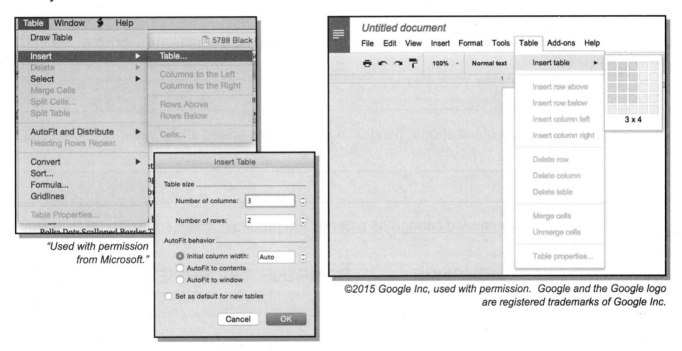

"Used with permission from Microsoft."

©2015 Google Inc, used with permission. Google and the Google logo are registered trademarks of Google Inc.

3. The chart should have 5 columns and 3 rows.

4. Your empty chart will appear on your page.

5. You can make adjustments by going back to **Table** on the menu bar. You can make the size of the cells different and you can add or delete rows and columns.

    Your chart should look like this:

TRIALS	1	2	3	4
12 INCH				
6 INCH				

6. Use the information you compiled on the previous pages to complete the chart.

 _____

MAKE A SIMPLE PENDULUM

JOURNAL ENTRY

1. What do you find most interesting about pendulums? _____

   _____

2. Have you noticed pendulums anywhere since you started this unit?   **YES   NO**

   Give two examples of pendulums.

   _____   _____

3. Based on your testing, which angle worked better for starting a pendulum in motion? **90° 60°**

   Why? _____

   _____

4. What was the effect of the shorter pendulum string on the speed and number of oscillations?

   _____

   _____

5. Does the time of the period change as a pendulum gradually loses energy, or does it stay
   the same?

   CHANGE   REMAINS THE SAME

   Explain. _____

   _____

   _____

6. Do you think it would have helped to have a third person on your team to do the recording?

   YES   NO

   Explain. _____

   _____

   _____

   _____

DESIGN PROCESS REVIEW—MAKE A SIMPLE PENDULUM

Share your observations, journal entries, and other documentation about your experiences
with simple pendulums in a class discussion led by your teacher.

ANGLES AND OSCILLATIONS

Teacher Preparation: Each trio of students will need one 12" pendulum. The objective will be to count the number of oscillations of the pendulum when it is released at different degrees—**135°**, **90°**, **60°**, and **45°**. Try laminating the large protractor on page 55 or copying it onto heavy paper. Cut a hole in it so it can be added to the rod. After the first round of testing, students will double the weight of the bob and retest. This may take two or three 40-minute sessions to complete.

TEAM MATERIALS
- rod and 12" pendulum from Unit 2, Activity 1
- large paper clips (4 more per pendulum)
- masking tape or duct tape
- protractors
- rulers
- stopwatches or 1-minute timers

SET UP THE PENDULUM

1. Use a 12" pendulum from Activity 1. Have protractors available.

2. Tape the rods between two desks or tables. There should be at least 18" of free space between the desks.

3. Check the length of the pendulums. The fishing line should be 12" long from the rod to the bob.

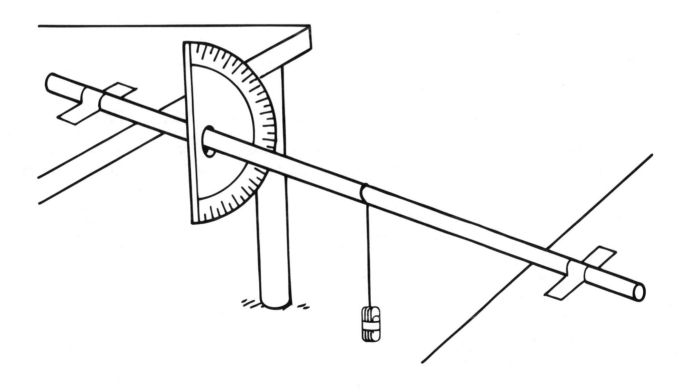

NAME _____

ANGLES AND OSCILLATIONS

Directions: Work in groups of three for this activity. Read through ALL the directions for the activity before you begin. You will be filling in the results in charts on pages 63–66 to show times and observations on types of movements.

12" PENDULUM—OSCILLATIONS AT 135 DEGREES

1. Find 135° on the protractor to the right. Mark that angle.

2. **TEAMMATE 1:** Carefully lift the bob while keeping the line taut so that it is above the rod at an angle of about 135°. Make sure there is nothing in the way of the path of the pendulum.

   TEAMMATE 2: Get ready to time the pendulum's oscillations for 1 minute.

   TEAMMATE 3: Get ready to record the results on the charts that are on pages 63 and 64.

3. **TEAMMATE 1:** Prepare to count the oscillations while your teammate is timing the pendulum.

   TEAMMATE 2: Say "**GO**," and start the timer. Keep timing until the pendulum stops moving or until you hit the 1-minute mark.

   TEAMMATE 3: Record the results on the charts on pages 63 and 64.

4. Do three trials using the steps above. Each teammate should have a turn timing the pendulum and a turn releasing the pendulum at 135° and counting the oscillations. Don't forget to put your initials in the circle next to your results on each page.

5. Use the chart on page 64 to describe how the bob behaves. Observe the bob. Does it make a smooth or an uneven swing?

6. Does the bob continue to swing above the line of the rod?   **YES   NO**

7. Take turns recording the number of oscillations in 1 minute on the chart that is on page 63. *Note:* If the oscillations stop before the minute is up, stop counting and note the time in the chart.

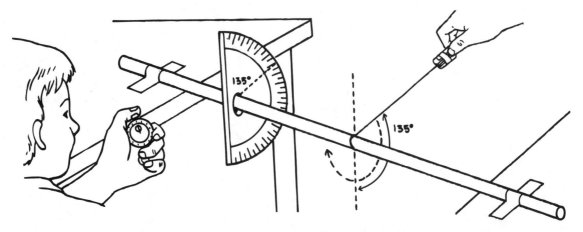

★ ★ ★ SAVE THE PENDULUMS FOR ACTIVITY 3 ★ ★ ★

 NAME _____

ANGLES AND OSCILLATIONS

Directions: Read ALL the directions first. Work in groups of three for this activity. Each teammate will do one trial at each angle. The initials of the person releasing the bob for each trial will go in the circle and he or she will log in his or her results on the charts here and on page 64.

1. Use the protractor to help you find the angles. Each teammate will do one trial for each angle.

2. Hold the bob at each angle and count and time the oscillations for 1 minute.

3. Log in the number of oscillations on the line below. Log your observations for each angle tested on page 64.

   Note: The pendulum may stop before the 1-minute time limit. If it does stop, write down how long it kept moving in the space under the line for the number of oscillations.

NUMBER OF OSCILLATIONS		
12" PENDULUM WITH 4-CLIP BOB		
TRIAL	**1ST TRIAL**	**2ND TRIAL**	**3RD TRIAL**
135°	_____ ◯	_____ ◯	_____ ◯
90°	_____ ◯	_____ ◯	_____ ◯
60°	_____ ◯	_____ ◯	_____ ◯
45°	_____ ◯	_____ ◯	_____ ◯

ANGLES AND OSCILLATIONS

Directions: Circle whether the bob moved in a smooth or uneven manner for each angle. Each observer should write his or her initials in the appropriate circle.

OBSERVATIONS—PATH OF THE 4-CLIP BOB			
TRIAL	**1ST TRIAL**	**2ND TRIAL**	**3RD TRIAL**
135°	SMOOTH UNEVEN ◯	SMOOTH UNEVEN ◯	SMOOTH UNEVEN ◯
90°	SMOOTH UNEVEN ◯	SMOOTH UNEVEN ◯	SMOOTH UNEVEN ◯
60°	SMOOTH UNEVEN ◯	SMOOTH UNEVEN ◯	SMOOTH UNEVEN ◯
45°	SMOOTH UNEVEN ◯	SMOOTH UNEVEN ◯	SMOOTH UNEVEN ◯

ANGLES AND OSCILLATIONS

Directions: Work in groups of three for this activity. Read through ALL the directions for the activity before you begin. Each teammate will do one trial at each angle at the new weight. Results and observations will be logged in on the charts here and on page 66.

1. Make the bob heavier by adding four more large paper clips to it.

2. Hold the 8-clip bob at each angle and take turns counting and timing the oscillations.

3. Each teammate will do one trial for each angle. Always stop at 1 minute.

4. Log in the number of oscillations below and observations on page 66 for each angle tested.

   Note: The pendulum may stop before the 1-minute time limit. If it does stop, write down how long it kept moving in the space under the line for the number of oscillations.

12" PENDULUM WITH 8-CLIP BOB			
TRIAL	1ST TRIAL	2ND TRIAL	3RD TRIAL
135°	_____ ◯	_____ ◯	_____ ◯
90°	_____ ◯	_____ ◯	_____ ◯
60°	_____ ◯	_____ ◯	_____ ◯
45°	_____ ◯	_____ ◯	_____ ◯

ANGLES AND OSCILLATIONS

Directions: Circle whether the bob traveled smoothly or unevenly for each angle. Add your initials.

OBSERVATIONS—PATH OF THE 8-CLIP BOB			
TRIAL	1ST TRIAL	2ND TRIAL	3RD TRIAL
135°	SMOOTH UNEVEN ◯	SMOOTH UNEVEN ◯	SMOOTH UNEVEN ◯
90°	SMOOTH UNEVEN ◯	SMOOTH UNEVEN ◯	SMOOTH UNEVEN ◯
60°	SMOOTH UNEVEN ◯	SMOOTH UNEVEN ◯	SMOOTH UNEVEN ◯
45°	SMOOTH UNEVEN ◯	SMOOTH UNEVEN ◯	SMOOTH UNEVEN ◯

KEEP TESTING!

1. What happens when you hold the bob straight up (180°) above the ground? _____

   _____

2. How high (which angle) can you hold a bob and still get an even—not jerky—swing?

   _____

Ⓝ Ⓐ Ⓜ Ⓔ _____

ANGLES AND OSCILLATIONS

JOURNAL ENTRY

1. What surprised you most about the swing of the pendulum at 135°? _____

_____

_____

2. Do you think the *length* of the bob affects the swing?   **YES   NO**

   Explain your answer. _____

   _____

3. Do you think the *weight* of the bob affects the swing?   **YES   NO**

   Explain your answer. _____

   _____

4. Did the number of oscillations differ very much between the 4-clip bob and the 8-clip bob?

   YES   NO   SOME

   Explain your answer. _____

   _____

5. What other variation would you like to try? _____

   Explain why. _____

   _____

6. Was it easier or more difficult to have a third person on the team to help log in the results?

   EASIER   HARDER

   Explain. _____

   _____

DESIGN PROCESS REVIEW—ANGLES AND OSCILLATIONS

Share your observations, journal entries, and other documentation about your experiences releasing pendulums at different angles in a class discussion led by your teacher.

 NAME _____

WORKING WITH TWO PENDULUMS

Directions: Work in groups of three for this activity. Read through ALL the directions for the activity before you begin. You will be working with two pendulums, moving them at the same time. This process will create a *transfer of energy*—it occurs from one pendulum to another when one or more pendulums are in motion. That transfer, carried along the rod, will occur until all motion ends.

TEAM MATERIALS

- fishing line—8-pound test or higher
- large paper clips
- masking tape or duct tape
- protractors

- rods, 36" or longer
- rulers
- stopwatches or timers

Optional: Reuse the rods and 12" pendulums with 4 large clips from previous activities.

TWO PENDULUM SET UP

1. Tape the rod between two desks. There should be 18" or more of free space between desks.

2. Create or reuse two 12" pendulums using bobs with four large paper clips. Check the length so that the pendulums are both 12" long from the rod to the bob.

3. Arrange the two pendulums on the bar so that they do not swing into each other or into the sides of the desks.

   How far apart did you place the two pendulums? _____

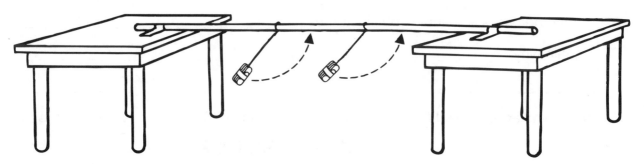

4. Decide which pendulum will be Pendulum 1 and which will be Pendulum 2. Label them.

5. Time each pendulum to find the period.

   Period for Pendulum 1: _____   **Period for Pendulum 2:** _____

6. What do you think a *transfer of energy* in the pendulums might look like? Share your thoughts and then test out your theory in the next activity.

_____

_____

_____

NAME _____

WORKING WITH TWO PENDULUMS

Directions: Work in groups of three for this activity. Read through ALL the directions for the activity before you begin. Before testing, decide which teammate will do each job on the team.

TESTING THE PENDULUMS

1. Fill in the name of each teammate and review each job.

   TEAMMATE 1 _____ will say, "**GO**," and time the test (3 minutes or less).

   TEAMMATE 2 _____ will hold and release Pendulum 1 and count the oscillations.

   TEAMMATE 3 _____ will hold and release Pendulum 2 and count the oscillations.

2. Each bob should be held taut at about a 60° angle. Mark 60° on the protractor.

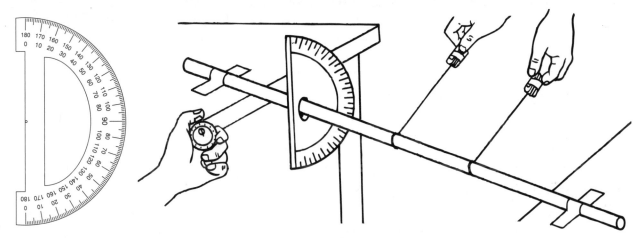

3. When **Teammate 1** says, "**GO**," **Teammate 2** and **Teammate 3** will simultaneously release the pendulums.

4. Record the number of oscillations in one minute.

   PERIOD FOR PENDULUM 1 _____ **oscillations in one minute**

   PERIOD FOR PENDULUM 2 _____ **oscillations in one minute**

5. Continue observing the pendulums until they are both inert. How long did it take?

   _____

6. Describe the movements of the pendulums. Did they move in the same way or differently?

   _____

   _____

   _____

WORKING WITH TWO PENDULUMS

Directions: Work in groups of three for this activity. Read through ALL the directions for the activity before you begin. You will be making and testing a heavier bob.

ADDING WEIGHT

1. Add four more paper clips to Pendulum 2 to double the weight of the bob.

2. Observe how the two pendulums work when let go at the same time.

   TEAMMATE 1 will say "**GO**" and will time the test. Call out 1 minute, 2 minutes, and stop at 3 minutes.

   TEAMMATE 2 will hold and release Pendulum 1 and will count and record the oscillations.

   At the same time, **TEAMMATE 3** will hold and release Pendulum 2 and will count and record the oscillations.

3. What do you observe when the pendulums are first released?

   _____

   _____

4. What do you observe after 1 minute?

   _____

   _____

5. What do you observe after 2 minutes?

   _____

   _____

6. What do you observe at the 3-minute mark?

   _____

   _____

7. Was the transfer of energy different when the two bobs had different weights?

   _____

   _____

   _____

 _____

WORKING WITH TWO PENDULUMS

JOURNAL ENTRY

1. Discuss any problems you encountered setting up the two-pendulum activity. Give details.

   _____

   _____

   _____

2. Do two pendulums of the same length and weight always swing simultaneously (at the same time)?

   _____

   _____

   _____

3. What happens as two pendulums swing on the same rod? Describe the *transfer of energy*.

   _____

   _____

   _____

4. What is the most interesting thing you learned about pendulums?

   _____

   _____

   _____

5. Can you think of any places you have seen or used pendulums since you started this unit?

   _____

   _____

   _____

DESIGN PROCESS REVIEW—WORKING WITH TWO PENDULUMS

Share your observations, journal entries, and other documentation about your experiences with working two pendulums at the same time in a class discussion led by your teacher.

 NAME _____

CHALLENGE: CREATE A PENDULUM WAVE

WHAT IS A PENDULUM WAVE?

Some say it is art, and some say it is physics. A *pendulum wave* uses motion to create a special effect. The pendulums move in and out of sync and create a variety of wave patterns. Many pendulums of different lengths are combined and simultaneously set in motion.

Teacher Preparation: Present this challenge as a large group or whole class activity. The objective will be to work together to create a pendulum wave.

1. Decide ahead of time how your class might best approach this project based on class size, ability, and available materials.

   ✓ How many pendulums should the first wave have? The activity will work with a minimum of 6 and a maximum of 16 pendulums using the materials listed. A longer rod might work better if students want to add more pendulums.

   ✓ Should the wave be checked at intervals to see if it works?

   ✓ Should more than one wave be attempted by groups of students, or should this be a whole class project?

2. Set aside a time for students to view one of the suggested Pendulum Wave videos during the Brainstorm/Research period. Try one of the suggested videos or have students do their own research with supervision.

   Pendulum Wave Demonstration
   https://www.youtube.com/watch?v=YhMiuzyU1ag

   The Pendulum Wave Machine
   http://www.eepybird.com/experiments/pendulumwave/

3. Gather materials from past activities and new materials as needed, including the following:

   ☐ Weights of some kind to use for the bobs. They should all be the same. You might try nuts, washers, wooden beads, or other objects.

   ☐ rod, 36" or longer

   ☐ duct tape

   ☐ fishing line—8 pound test or higher

   ☐ rulers (cm)

   ☐ yardstick or other 36" board

POSSIBLE PENDULUM LENGTHS FOR A 9 PENDULUM WAVE

Encourage students to come as close as possible. Many adjustments may need to be made to get each pendulum the correct length.

LENGTH IN CENTIMETERS	35.7	33.0	30.6	28.5	26.6	24.8	23.2	21.8	20.5
PENDULUM	1	2	3	4	5	6	7	8	9

REMINDER: The fishing line for each pendulum should be cut longer. The *suggested* lengths are for individual pendulums in the wave.

_____

CHALLENGE: CREATE A PENDULUM WAVE

Directions: Each team or small group will add a pendulum of a specific measurement to a rod.

BRAINSTORM: Think about what you have learned about pendulums. What do you think would happen if you put *more* than two pendulums on the same rod?

Have you seen that done before?   **YES   NO**

_____

_____

_____

RESEARCH: Find out more about pendulum waves and the pendulum lengths needed to create a wave.

Fact 1: _____

_____

Fact 2: _____

_____

DESIGN THE SOLUTION: Sketch your plan here. List and label the lengths of the pendulums your team has chosen to try, or use the pendulums lengths suggested by your teacher.

LENGTH OF PENDULUMS

1 _____

2 _____

3 _____

4 _____

5 _____

6 _____

7 _____

8 _____

9 _____

CHALLENGE: CREATE A PENDULUM WAVE

BUILD: Use the materials you have gathered to assemble a pendulum wave.

Question: Will you try out the wave after every two or three pendulum additions to check it, or will you add all the pendulums before testing?

☐ **FEW AT A TIME**   ☐ **ALL AT ONCE**

EVALUATE: Think about your assembly and testing.

Describe problems that occurred during construction.

_____

_____

_____

Did your pendulum wave work as you planned?   **YES   NO**

Explain: _____

_____

_____

MODIFY: Engineering design is the way materials are assembled for a successful project. What adjustments will/did you make to get the pendulums to work together to create the wave?

_____

_____

_____

SHARE: Describe the results of your project.

_____

_____

_____

How many wave patterns could you see?

_____

_____

_____

Soap Science

5 sessions: 1 session for each activity (approximately 1 to $1\frac{1}{2}$ hours per session)

Focus: Physical Science—properties of soap film, properties of water

CONNECTIONS AND SUGGESTIONS

SCIENCE—Students will explore bubbles and combine everyday materials to create soap film. They will be examining the characteristics of soap film—they will observe, define, and compare the properties of bubbles. Students will also try to determine why bubbles float and more importantly, why they usually float up.

TECHNOLOGY—Students may use computers or tablets to review approved videos and do additional research on bubbles and soap film. Additionally, they may photograph or record their observations and responses as they create a variety of bubble wands. They may use computers to document their observations and experiences and/or to create charts.

ENGINEERING—Students will be working with elements of design to construct a variety of two-dimensional and three-dimensional geometric figures that they will use as bubble frames or wands. They will compare the bubble wands, make improvements, and test and retest them to make the best bubbles (biggest, longest lasting, etc.).

MATH—Geometry concepts in this unit involve the creation of straw models of two- and three-dimensional geometric shapes and the measurement of angles and lengths. The activities require students to measure using both standard and metric rulers. Students will use protractors to measure a variety of angles and to help them with construction and testing.

DISCUSSION PROMPT: What do we know about bubbles?

A bubble is a thin film of liquid surrounding a gas—in this case, air. Bubbles are usually spheres and these spherical shapes tend to float. Bubbles you blow float up because the air inside the bubble is warmer than the air outside. A bubble made with a wand will also float up if there is a breeze.

The soap bubbles in our activities will be made up of a thin layer of water surrounded by two layers of soap film. As time passes, this film gets thinner and thinner, causing the bubble to pop.

Bubbles get their color as light passes through them. This is called *iridescence*. The colors you see are caused when light hits the bubble. This light might reflect off the outer layer to create colors. The light can also enter the film and bounce off the inner layer, or it might just bounce between the two soap film layers. The thinner the wall of the bubble is, the more colors you will see. So, a bubble is its most colorful just before it pops.

SOAP SCIENCE

UNIT MATERIALS (for a class of 30 to 35)

- ☐ bus trays or dish pans (4 students per tub)
- ☐ Dawn® liquid soap
- ☐ fishing line (8-pound test or higher—20 pound test is thicker and easier to tie)
- ☐ glycerin (found in drug stores) or light cooking oil
- ☐ measuring cups
- ☐ protractors
- ☐ quart container
- ☐ rulers and measuring tapes or yardsticks

- ☐ scissors
- ☐ spatulas/spoons
- ☐ thin, coated wire (20–22 gauge)
- ☐ thin straws (coffee stirrers) and regular straws
- ☐ water
- ☐ wooden dowels or wooden barbeque skewers (grocery stores)
- ☐ yarn, string, or twine

> **About the Wire:** 20–22 gauge bell wire can be found in hardware stores and is easy for students to manipulate. Other types of coated wire will also work as long as they are thin. Cables from older TVs can be separated and used as well—if you can find them!

FIND OUT MORE

Bubbleologist Geoff Akins teaches kids to be positive through his bubble shows
http://www.nbcchicago.com/news/local/Bubbleologist_Teaches_Kids_Life_Lessons.html

This Bubble Artist's Amazing Bubble Skills Will Blow You Away!
https://www.youtube.com/watch?v=QseWXpkaGTY

BUBBLEOLOGY Show: Keith Johnson Explores How Soap Bubbles Work & What's New They Can Do
https://www.youtube.com/watch?v=8_5AsgMM4CE

Safety Note: All websites should be checked prior to student viewing to be certain that content is appropriate.

SOAP SCIENCE VOCABULARY

2-dimensional (2D)—having a form with length and width
Example: a square

3-dimensional (3D)—having a form with length, width, and depth
Example: a cube

apex—point where all faces of a pyramid meet; the highest point

base—a thing or part on which something rests

bubble—a thin sphere of liquid (like soap film) enclosing air or another gas

edge—the line where two faces of a solid figure meet

exterior angle—an angle formed outside a geometric shape

face—a plane figure that serves as one side of a solid figure

film—a thin layer on the surface of something

flexible—capable of bending easily without breaking

interior angle—an angle within a geometric figure

iridescent—displaying a rainbow of colors that seem to move or shimmer

protractor—a device for measuring angles

solution—a special type of mixture consisting of two or more items mixed together that form one substance (*Example:* dish soap and water)

spherical—having a round shape that looks like a ball

vertex—a corner point

vertices—plural of vertex

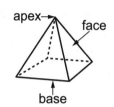

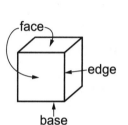

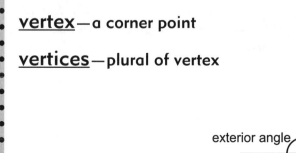

NAME _____

SOAP SCIENCE

2-DIMENSIONAL SHAPES—PLANE FIGURES

Two-dimensional shapes are flat. Some have sides, others do not.

Directions: Trace the outline of each shape.

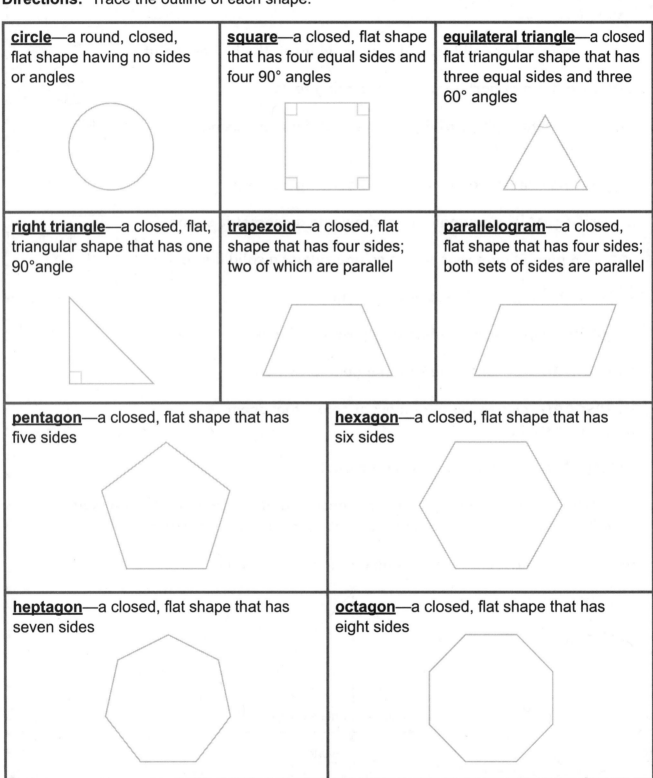

circle—a round, closed, flat shape having no sides or angles	**square**—a closed, flat shape that has four equal sides and four 90° angles	**equilateral triangle**—a closed flat triangular shape that has three equal sides and three 60° angles
right triangle—a closed, flat, triangular shape that has one 90°angle	**trapezoid**—a closed, flat shape that has four sides; two of which are parallel	**parallelogram**—a closed, flat shape that has four sides; both sets of sides are parallel

pentagon—a closed, flat shape that has five sides

hexagon—a closed, flat shape that has six sides

heptagon—a closed, flat shape that has seven sides

octagon—a closed, flat shape that has eight sides

SOAP SCIENCE

3-DIMENSIONAL SHAPES—SOLID FIGURES

Three-dimensional shapes are solid figures, not flat ones. Some solid figures have bases and sides, others do not.

Directions: Trace the outline of each solid shape. Use one color for the bases and another color for the faces. *Note:* Your colors may overlap.

cone—a solid shape that has 1 base that is a circle and a curved surface for a side, which meets in a point at the top.	**cylinder**—a solid shape that has 2 bases that are circles and one curved side.	**sphere**—a solid shape that is round and looks like a ball.
	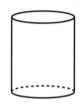	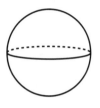

prism—a solid shape that has 2 indentical, parallel bases. A prism is named by the shape of its bases. Here are two examples:

square prism (cube)—a solid shape that has 2 square bases and 4 other square faces. All six faces have the same dimensions.	**triangular prism**—a solid shape that has 2 triangular bases (or sides) and 3 other rectangular faces.
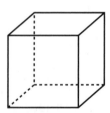	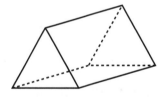

pyramid—a solid shape that has 1 *base* that can be a variety of different shapes. It has a triangular *face* for each side of the base. These side faces form a point at the top or *apex*. Examples:

triangular pyramid (tetrahedron)—a solid shape that has 1 triangular base and 3 other triangular faces.	**square pyramid**—a solid shape that has 1 square base and 4 other triangular faces.	**rectangular pyramid**—a solid shape that has 1 rectangular base and 4 other triangular faces.
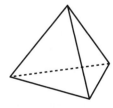	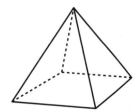	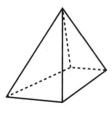

SOAP SCIENCE

Directions: Use the words in the Word Bank to label each 2D and 3D shape.

WORD BANK

circle	octagon	parallelogram	square	trapezoid
heptagon	pentagon	rectangular pyramid	square pyramid	triangle
hexagon	square prism	sphere	triangular pyramid	triangular prism

2-DIMENSIONAL SHAPES—Count the sides and write the number in the 2D shape.

 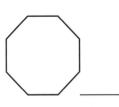 

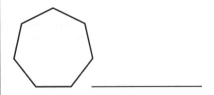 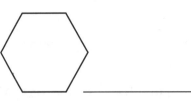 

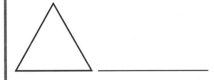 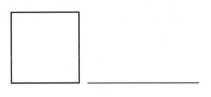 

3-DIMENSIONAL SHAPES—Count the faces and write the number in the 3D shape.

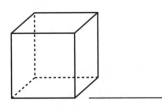 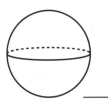 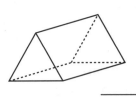

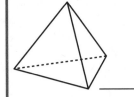 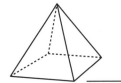 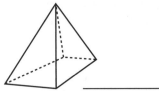

What is another name for a square prism? _____

SOAP SCIENCE

WHO KNEW?

HOLD A BUBBLE

HOLD A BUBBLE

Brenda was at the Bubble Festival, and she was excited. Everywhere she looked, people were blowing bubbles from big tubs that were filled with soap-bubble solutions. There were different kinds of wands and even a place where you could stand in a wading pool and have a giant bubble made around you!

Bubbles of all sizes were floating in the sky. They shimmered. The bubbles seemed to be many different colors. Some stuck together. They were popping all over the place as people tried to catch them. Brenda really wanted to hold a bubble, but how?

Just then, everyone was called to the main stage for the show. It was amazing. The "bubbleologist" made wonderful bubbles. She even made a square bubble in the middle of a group of bubble spheres. Then, she filled the square bubble with smoke!

The woman with the bubbles could hold them in her hand, and they did not pop. Brenda watched her very carefully. Finally, she noticed that the bubbleologist always dipped her hands in the soap-bubble solution before she touched a bubble. Could that be it? Brenda couldn't wait to try it.

1. After reading the passage, what do you think a "bubbleologist" is?

   _____

   _____

   _____

   Would you like to be a bubbleologist?   **YES   NO**

2. Why do you think dipping your hand in the soap-bubble solution will help hold a bubble? Explain.

   _____

   _____

3. List words to describe how a bubble looks.

   _____   _____   _____

4. List words to describe how a bubble moves.

   _____   _____   _____

5. Use the word *iridescent* in a descriptive sentence.

   _____

   _____

SOAP SCIENCE

BUBBLES

Sami and Joe were playing in the sand at the beach. They could see the foamy waves crashing against the shore. Joe asked, "Are those bubbles in the waves the same as the bubbles we blow?"

Sami, his sister, said, "No." She explained that the ocean was made of salt water, not soap! Joe was still curious and wondered about all the bubbles in the waves.

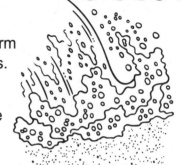

He decided to ask the lifeguard about them. The lifeguard explained that the pounding waves caused bubbles to form in the water. He explained that when a lot of bubbles bump together those bubbles form foam—much like the foam you get when you pour a soda into a glass.

Joe decided to see if he could make bubbles when he went to lunch. He did! First, he used a straw to blow bubbles in his water. Then, he poured a soda from a can into a glass and made so much foam that it overflowed. Then, he washed his hands. More bubbles!

1. List two or three things you do each day that make bubbles or foam.

   _____   _____   _____

2. Start a class chart of examples of bubbles. Use pictures, word cards, drawings, or other examples. Keep adding to the chart as you work on the unit.

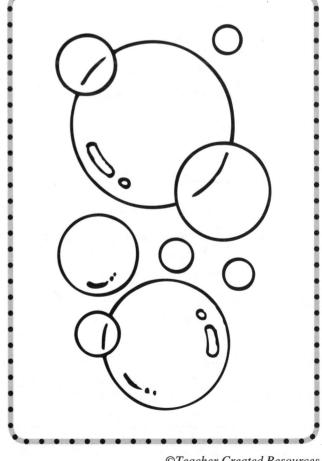

3. Try to find at least one picture of a bubble that shows it is *iridescent.*

4. Can you think of something else in nature that is iridescent? Describe it.

   _____

   _____

   _____

   _____

   _____

   _____

5. Use colored pencils to color the bubbles. Try to make them look iridescent.

 **NAME** _____

CREATING SOAP BUBBLES

Directions: Work in pairs to perform this first soap activity. Four students (two pairs) can share each tub. Take care with the measurements. Be as accurate as possible in measuring the ingredients for the solution and the lengths at the wires and straws.

TEAM MATERIALS

Soap-Bubble Solution (per tub)
- 4 ounces of Dawn® dish soap
- 2 ounces of glycerin or light cooking oil
- 2 quarts of water (distilled or tap)
- dish pan or bus tray
- measuring cups
- quart container
- spatula or large spoon

Other Materials
- thin, coated wire for each student (at least 6" in length)
- rulers and tape measures

Teacher Notes: If Dawn dish soap is not available, try Joy®. Do not use discount or dollar store dish soap. It tends to be too watery. Try distilled water if it is available. It seems to make longer lasting bubbles.

PREPARE THE SOAP-BUBBLE SOLUTION AND THE WAND

1. Pour 2 quarts of water into a pan or bus tray.

2. Add 4 ounces of Dawn dish soap to the water.

3. Add 2 ounces of glycerin or 2 ounces of light cooking oil.

4. Bend the six-inch wire into a circle with a one-inch diameter. The remaining wire will be the handle for the wire wand. The handle will be approximately 3 inches long.

5. Stir the soap-bubble solution thoroughly with the wire wand or a spoon.

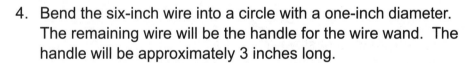

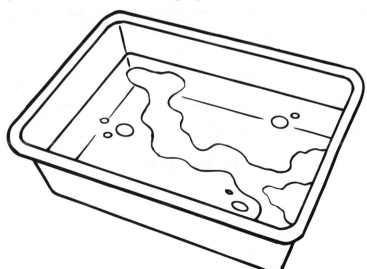

CREATING SOAP BUBBLES

WORKING WITH THE SOAP-BUBBLE SOLUTION AND THE WAND

1. Carefully, dip the wand into the solution and lift it out. Examine the "soap window" in the wire circle. What do you see?

   Is there movement?   **YES**   **NO**

   If yes, list some descriptive words to describe the movement.

   _____   _____   _____

   Are there different colors?   **YES**   **NO**   If so, add the colors to the circle above.

2. Dip the wand in the soap-bubble solution. Gently press a dry finger through the soap film. What happens?

   _____

   _____

   Wet your finger in the solution and try to put it through the soap film again. What happens this time?

   _____

3. Slowly *wave* the wand through the air several times. Describe what happens to the soap film.

   _____

   _____

   What happens if you wave rapidly instead of slowly?

   _____

4. Repeat the activity above but *blow* the soap film in the wire circle. Describe what happens when you blow on the soap film in the wand.

   _____

   _____

   Did you make one bubble or many bubbles? _____

   Does the size of the bubbles vary?   **YES**   **NO**

   If yes, how do the bubbles vary?

   _____

CREATING SOAP BUBBLES

SMALLER WANDS

1. First, make the wire circle of the wand smaller. Try wrapping it around a marker to help you get a smaller circle shape.

2. Dip the wand into the soap mixture. Wave the smaller wire wand or blow into it.

3. Do the bubbles appear to be larger or smaller than the bubbles from the first wand?

    LARGER   SMALLER

4. Did you get more bubbles, less bubbles, or about the same amount of bubbles using the smaller wand?

_____

LARGER WANDS

1. Next, form a circle with the wire and make it as large as you can. (*Note:* If more wire is available, you might wish to make an even larger circle.)

    What is the new diameter of the circle you made with the wire? _____

2. Dip the larger wire circle into the soapy solution. Wave the bubble wand or blow on the film to make a bubble.

    Does the circle wand work without a handle?   **YES   NO**

    Which method works better, waving or blowing? _____

3. Which size wand did you prefer? _____

4. Describe the shape, color, and movement of the bubbles.

_____

_____

_____

5. Look for two bubbles that are stuck together.

    Are the two bubbles the same size or is one larger?   **SAME   DIFFERENT**

Look Closely: See if you can find two bubbles that have a flat wall between them. Usually that means that the two bubbles were the same size when they touched.

If one bubble is smaller, it should push into the larger bubble, creating an indent instead of a flat wall. Draw the combinations you saw on the back of this page.

 NAME _____

CREATING SOAP BUBBLES

WANDS OF DIFFERENT SHAPES

1. Experiment with different-shaped wands. Bend a piece of 6"–8" wire into an irregular shape and twist the ends together.

2. In the sketch box, trace the shape you made.

3. Dip the new shape into the soap-bubble solution, lift it out, and blow gently on the soapy film inside the wire.

4. Did your shape wand work?   **YES   NO**

   Explain. _____

   _____

   _____

   Did you get more than one bubble?   **YES   NO**

   What shape bubbles does your wand make?   **SPHERES   CUBES   OTHER**

5. Compare your shape wand to the others in your group. Observe the bubbles each student can make. What do you notice?

   _____

   _____

6. Which type of designs do you think held the soap film best? _____

   What did they have in common?

   _____

   _____

7. Make one more wand based on your observations. Trace the wand in the sketch box.

8. Test the wand and describe how it worked.

   _____

   _____

   _____

★ **SAVE THE SOAP-BUBBLE SOLUTION AND BUS TRAYS FOR THE NEXT ACTIVITY** ★

CREATING SOAP BUBBLES

JOURNAL ENTRY

1. What did you learn about soap-bubble solutions in this activity? _____

   _____

   _____

   _____

2. Explain what *iridescent* means and give some examples. _____

   _____

   _____

   _____

3. What did you discover about bubble wands? _____

   _____

   _____

4. What shape wands seemed to make the best bubbles? _____

   Why do you think that shape worked so well? _____

   _____

   _____

5. Think about the bubbles you made using the two methods—waving and blowing. Was one method better for making bubbles than the other?

   _____

   Explain. _____

   _____

   _____

DESIGN PROCESS REVIEW—CREATING SOAP BUBBLES

Share your observations, journal entries, and other documentation about your bubble activity with your classmates in a discussion led by your teacher.

2D-SHAPE WANDS

TEACHER PREPARATION: Students may work in teams of two (pairs) as they carry out this activity, but each should make his or her own geometric bubble wands. Explain to students that they will be using the straws with wire or fishing line to make different, geometric-shaped wands for their soap bubble solutions. Encourage students to make constructions using both wire and fishing line. Perhaps one teammate can use wire and the other fishing line.

TEAM MATERIALS
- soap-bubble solution
- dishpans or bus trays
- fishing line (at least 8-lb. test) or wire (20–22 gauge)
- protractors
- rulers
- scissors
- thin straws

TEACHER NOTE: This project works with any straws, but stiff, inexpensive, thin straws (coffee stirrers) work well.

SQUARE WANDS

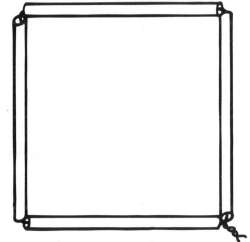

1. Use wire or fishing line to string four straws of equal length together. Twist the wire or tie the fishing line together.

2. You should now have a square shape. If you bend the figure slightly, it will form a parallelogram. Make a prediction. What shape will the bubble be?

_____

3. Stir the solution for a minute to fully mix the ingredients. Dip the square wand into the soap-bubble solution and carefully pull it out.

4. Try to make a bubble by gently moving the wand through the air or by blowing gently on the soap film in the wand.

5. Examine the bubbles formed by the square wand.

What shape are they? _____

What size are they?   **SMALL** (marble)   **MEDIUM** (ping pong ball)   **LARGE** (basketball)

Do bubbles form almost every time you dip into the soap-bubble solution?   **YES   NO**

Describe the way your bubbles come out of the wand.

_____

_____

NAME _____

2D-SHAPE WANDS

TRIANGULAR WANDS

EQUILATERAL TRIANGLE WAND

1. Measure and cut three straws to be 5" or 6" in length. All three should be the same size.

2. Use the wire or fishing line to string the three straws together.

3. Twist the wire together or tie the fishing line to create the equilateral triangle.

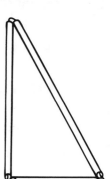

RIGHT TRIANGLE WAND

1. Now, make a right triangle. Use three straws cut to different lengths—3", 4", and 5".

2. Use the wire or fishing line to string the three straws together.

3. Twist the wire together or tie the fishing line to create the right triangle.

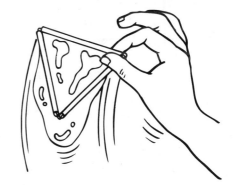

TEST THE TRIANGLE WANDS

1. Pull each wand through the soap-bubble solution and hold it up. Do you have a soap film across the triangle wands? If so, go on to the next step, if not, dip the wands again.

2. *Wave* each triangle wand through the air and describe what happens.

   _____

   _____

   _____

   _____

3. Dip the wands again and this time, gently *blow* on each wand. Does the blowing method make similar bubbles to the waving method?

YES   NO

   Explain. _____

   _____

   _____

   _____

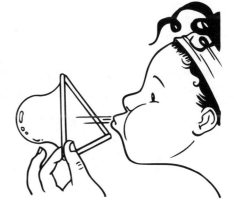

2D-SHAPE WANDS

TEACHER PREPARATION: Each team of students will create a two-dimensional wand in a geometric shape using straws and wire or fishing line. The dimensions are listed below each shape.

1. Encourage students to work with both wire and fishing line when constructing different shapes and to compare each material. Is one more useful or manageable than the other?

2. Have students take a poll before cutting their straws to see which team is making each shape.

3. Ask students to fill in their names or initials in the shape they will be making and to double check the number of sides it has before beginning construction.

4. Make certain that each shape shown below will be made by at least one team.

CONSTRUCTING 2D-SHAPE WANDS

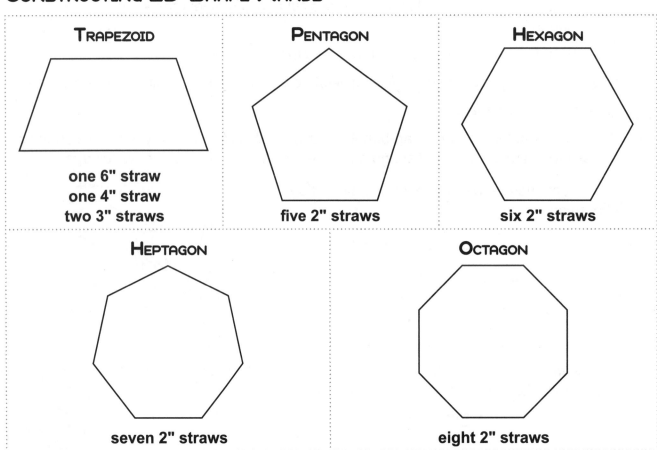

TRAPEZOID
one 6" straw
one 4" straw
two 3" straws

PENTAGON
five 2" straws

HEXAGON
six 2" straws

HEPTAGON
seven 2" straws

OCTAGON
eight 2" straws

Directions: Follow the suggested dimensions above to make a geometric-shaped wand with your partner. The wand will be two dimensional, which means it will be flat.

1. Cut and measure your straws to make the 2D-shape wand.

2. Think carefully about how much wire or fishing line you will need to make your 2D shape. Do your calculations in the frame on the right.

3. Work together and assemble each 2D-shape wand.

4. Once your shape is complete, use a protractor to measure the angles of your shape and fill in the worksheet on the next page.

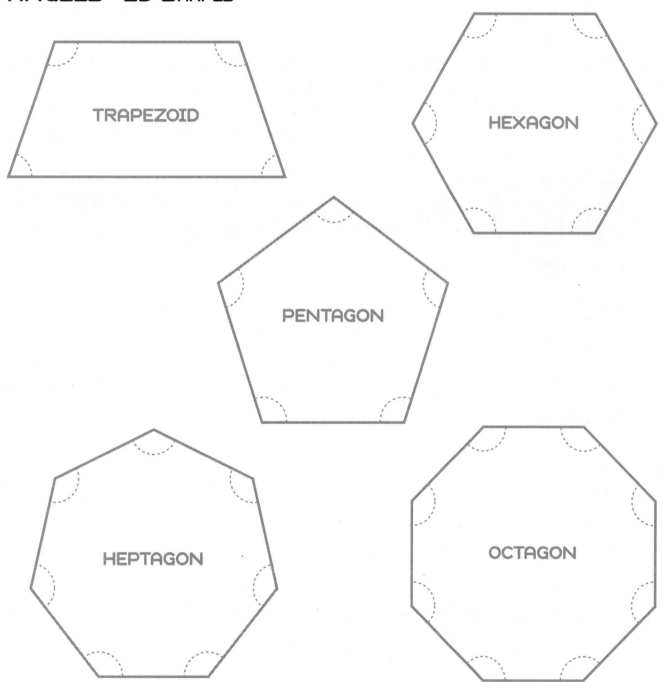

N A M E _____

2D-SHAPE WANDS

Directions: Measure the angles of the two-dimensional shape you created.

1. Use a protractor to measure the *interior angles* of the wand before you use it.

2. Below, record the degrees in your 2D shape.

3. Share the angle information with the other teams to fill in the rest of the shapes. Do this before using and sharing wands.

ANGLES—2D SHAPES

NAME _____

2D-SHAPE WANDS

USING 2D-SHAPE WANDS

1. Take turns using your team's shape wand. Which method works better?

   WAVING   BLOWING   NO DIFFERENCE

2. Does your team's wand work well?   **YES   NO**

   What adjustments do you need to make?

   _____

   _____

3. Retry the wand after the adjustments are made. Did you notice an improvement? **YES NO**

4. Trade wands with other teams. Use each shape wand in the soap-bubble solution at least once and then answer the questions below.

   Note whether waving or blowing worked better. If both methods worked the same, write "same."

   How many bubbles did your wand make? **0**, **1**, **few**, or **many**

2D-SHAPE WAND TESTS			
WAND SHAPE	WAVE OR BLOW	BUBBLE SHAPE	HOW MANY BUBBLES
TRAPEZOID ⬭			
PENTAGON ⬠			
HEXAGON ⬡			
HEPTAGON ⬡			
OCTAGON ⯃			

5. Did one wand style make more bubbles than the others?   **YES   NO**

   If so, which one(s) worked better? _____

   _____

6. Were the bubbles the same shape as the wands?   **YES   NO**

   If no, explain. _____

7. Which of the geometric figures do you think made the biggest bubbles?

   _____

★ SAVE THE SOAP-BUBBLE SOLUTION AND BUS TRAYS FOR THE NEXT ACTIVITY ★

2D-SHAPE WANDS

JOURNAL ENTRY

1. What do you think is the main difference between making a circular wand and one with sides?

_____

_____

_____

2. Which two-dimensional shape made the best bubbles for you? _____
What made you think so? Was it how long they lasted or how large they were? Explain.

_____

_____

_____

3. Compare working with fishing line to working with the wire to construct your shapes.
What differences did you notice?

_____

_____

_____

4. What colors and designs did you see in your bubbles before they burst?

_____

_____

_____

5. Did the bubbles you made from the wands that had corners
work the same way as the rounded wands?   **YES   NO**

   Explain. _____

_____

_____

DESIGN PROCESS REVIEW—2D-SHAPE WANDS

Share your observations, journal entries, and other documentation about your 2D wands with your classmates in a discussion led by your teacher.

_____

3D-SHAPE WANDS

Directions: Work in teams of two (pairs) to make 3D bubble frames (wands). Continue using straws with wire or fishing line, or a combination of the two materials. These three-dimensional bubble frames will have *faces, bases,* and *edges.* These 3D geometric-shaped wands will also be tested in the soap bubble solution.

TEAM MATERIALS

- dishpans or bus trays
- fishing line (at least 8-lb. test)
- protractors
- rulers
- scissors
- soap-bubble solution from Activity 1 and 2
- thin straws
- wire (20–22 gauge)

TEACHER NOTE: This project works with any straws, but inexpensive, thin straws or coffee stirrers (sold in boxes) work well.

MAKE AND TEST A TRIANGULAR PYRAMID WAND

A triangular pyramid is also called a *tetrahedron*. It has four triangular faces—one face forms the base, and the other three form the sides. The sides come together on top and form a point called the *apex*.

1. Make the triangular pyramid using 6 straws of equal size.

   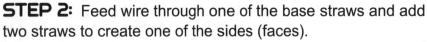

   STEP 1: Create a base by feeding wire or fishing line through 3 straws. Twist the wire together or tie the fishing line to form a triangle.

   STEP 2: Feed wire through one of the base straws and add two straws to create one of the sides (faces).

   STEP 3: Do Step 2 for the remaining two base straws to create the second and third side.

   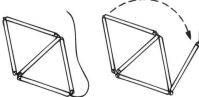

   STEP 4: Connect the three sides at the top to form a triangular pyramid or tetrahedron.

2. Dip the triangular pyramid into the soap-bubble solution. You may have to dip each face of the triangular pyramid separately until all 4 faces have a soap film.

3. Blow gently on the figure. What happened?

   _____

4. Wave the figure slowly through the air. What happened?

   _____

5. Which method seems to work better for this wand? **BLOW   WAVE   NO DIFFERENCE**

   Explain. _____

   _____

3D-SHAPE WANDS

Directions: Work in teams of two (pairs). Continue using straws with wire or fishing line to make more complex wands.

WORKING WITH TRIANGULAR PRISMS

Directions: Compare the two 3D shapes below and fill in the chart. Then, make a triangular prism wand and test it.

3D SHAPES	TRIANGULAR PYRAMID	TRIANGULAR PRISM
How many sides or faces?		
How many bases?		

Compare the two 3D shapes. What is the biggest difference you noticed? _____

_____

MAKE AND TEST A TRIANGULAR PRISM BUBBLE FRAME

1. Gather straws, fishing line or wire, scissors, and a ruler.

2. Cut six 4" straws and three 6" straws.

3. Each teammate (in pair) will make one equilateral triangle base using three 4" straws connected with thin wire or fishing line. These will create the top and bottom of your prism.

4. Connect 8" pieces of fishing line or wire to each corner of one triangle (bottom). Feed one piece of fishing line or wire through a 6" long straw and connect it to one corner of the second equilateral triangle (top).

5. Connect the remaining two 6" straws to the triangles in order to complete the prism. Check the prism to make certain it is sturdy.

6. Take turns dipping the triangular prism into the soap-bubble solution. You may have to dip several times to cover all the faces.

7. Describe how the soap arranges itself in the wand. _____

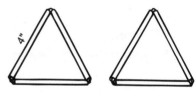

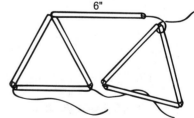

3D-SHAPE WANDS

Directions: Work in teams of two (pairs). Continue using straws and wire or fishing line to construct more complex wands. Use the illustrations to help guide your construction.

MAKING A SQUARE-BASED PYRAMID

Diagram 1

1. Gather straws, fishing line or wire, scissors, and a ruler to construct a square-based pyramid.

2. Cut eight 4" straws.

3. Arrange four 4" straws for the base and connect them with wire or fishing line. (See Diagram 1.)

4. Connect a length of wire or fishing line to each corner of the square.

5. Feed each line through a straw and lay them flat.

6. Gather two of the straws and tie them together to form a point. Do the same thing with the remaining two straws. (See Diagram 2.)

7. Connect the two straw triangles at the top to construct the pyramid. Make sure that the structure is sound.

Diagram 2

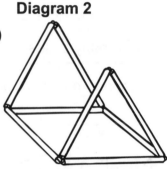

TEST THE SQUARE-BASED PYRAMID

1. Take turns dipping the pyramid bubble frame into the soap-bubble solution. You may have to dip the pyramid several times to cover all the faces.

2. Record what you see. What happens when you blow on the square-based pyramid or wave it through the air?

_____

_____

_____

3. Try dipping your hand in the solution and then gently pushing it through one of the faces.

Can you get your finger in the shape wand without popping the soap film?

Your hand?　**YES**　**NO**

YES　**NO**

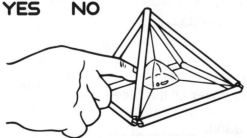

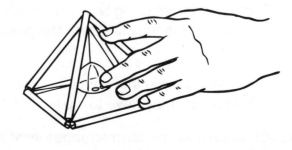

★ SAVE THE SOAP-BUBBLE SOLUTION AND BUS TRAYS FOR THE NEXT ACTIVITY ★

3D-SHAPE WANDS

JOURNAL ENTRY

1. Which 3D shape made the best bubbles for you? _____

   What made you think so? Was it how long they lasted or how large they were? Explain.

   _____

   _____

2. What was the most difficult part of the 3D construction of your wands? _____

   _____

   _____

   _____

3. What technique did you use to cover all the faces of the solid shape with soap film?

   _____

   _____

   _____

4. Why do you think it is easier to put a wet hand through soap film than a dry hand?

   _____

   _____

   _____

5. Why do you think bubbles always form a sphere, no matter what shape of bubble wand you use?

   _____

   _____

   _____

DESIGN PROCESS REVIEW—3D-SHAPE WANDS

Share your observations, journal entries, and other documentation about your 3D wands with your classmates in a discussion led by your teacher.

 NAME _____

FLEXIBLE BUBBLE WANDS

Directions: Work in teams of two (pairs). Construct two flexible bubble wands using yarn or twine with straws. One teammate will use the thin straws used in previous activities and one teammate will use larger straws. Use the illustrations to help guide your construction.

> **TEAM MATERIALS**
> - dishpans or bus trays
> - regular straws
> - rulers or yardsticks
> - scissors
> - soap-bubble solution
> - thin straws (coffee stirrers)
> - twine, yarn, string, or fishing line
> - wooden skewer

CONSTRUCT A FLEXIBLE BUBBLE WAND

1. Cut a piece of twine, yarn, string, or fishing line about 2 feet long.

2. Use a thin straw or wooden skewer to push the twine, yarn, or fishing line through first one wide straw and then a second wide straw. Tie the material securely.

3. Was it easy or difficult to push the line through the straw? **EASY   DIFFICULT**

   Did you use a different method? **YES   NO**

   If yes, explain. _____

   _____

4. Arrange the 2 straws so that they are handles on both sides of the bubble wand. Draw your wand.

5. Explain why this wand would be called a *flexible* wand. _____

   _____

   _____

FLEXIBLE BUBBLE WAND

TEST THE FLEXIBLE BUBBLE WANDS

1. Make sure that the soap-bubble solution is stirred thoroughly.

2. Take turns holding the straws of a flexible bubble wand and dipping it into the soap-bubble solution. Your hands will get wet!

3. Pull out the bubble wand and gently pull it through the air. Describe what happens and how large the bubble is.

_____

_____

4. Illustrate your bubble(s) and bubble wand in the frame.

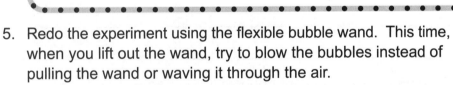

5. Redo the experiment using the flexible bubble wand. This time, when you lift out the wand, try to blow the bubbles instead of pulling the wand or waving it through the air.

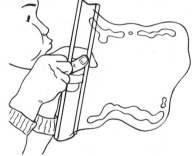

Describe how it worked. _____

_____

_____

6. Compare the two methods for making bubbles. Was there a difference in the bubbles you made when you blew the bubbles instead of waving the wand? Explain.

_____

_____

_____

★ SAVE THE SOAP-BUBBLE SOLUTION AND BUS TRAYS FOR THE NEXT ACTIVITY ★

 NAME _____

FLEXIBLE BUBBLE WANDS

JOURNAL ENTRY

1. What differences did you notice between the flexible wand with the regular straws and the wand with the thin straws?

   _____

   _____

   _____

2. Did the type of line (string, yarn, etc.) seem to matter in construction?   **YES   NO**

   Explain. _____

   _____

   _____

3. What was the most interesting part of using a flexible wand? _____

   _____

   _____

4. Of all the wands you made, which was your favorite? _____

   Explain. _____

   _____

   _____

5. Use colored pencils to draw and color iridescent bubbles in the frame.

DESIGN PROCESS REVIEW—FLEXIBLE BUBBLE WANDS

Share your observations, journal entries, and other documentation about making and using flexible wands with your classmates in a discussion led by your teacher.

CHALLENGE: MAKE SUPER BUBBLES

Directions: Work with a partner or small group. Make a bubble wand of your own design. Plan on using materials from activities in the unit and other, teacher-approved materials from the classroom or recycling area. Work with a partner or small group to test, adjust, and observe each other's creations.

BRAINSTORM: Think about what you have learned about soap film and bubble wands. Was there a wand design you wanted to try?

_____

Would you like to make larger bubbles, longer bubbles, or many tiny bubbles?

_____

What is your goal for this challenge? _____

_____

Will you need to do additional research? **YES**   **NO**

If so, what research do you want to do? _____

_____

DESIGN THE SOLUTION: Sketch your design here. Add notes as needed.

[sketch box]

BUILD: Briefly describe how you plan to build your Super Bubble Wand. _____

_____

What materials do you plan to use?

_____ _____ _____

_____ _____ _____

_____ _____ _____

CHALLENGE: MAKE SUPER BUBBLES

EVALUATE: Did your Super Bubble Wand work as you planned?   **YES   NO**

Was it easy to manipulate?   **YES   NO**

Explain. _____

_____

How large were the bubbles? _____

What size ball were the bubbles most like?

PING PONG BALL   TENNIS BALL   BASKETBALL   BEACH BALL

Did the bubbles last a longer time or pop right away? _____

_____

MODIFY: What adjustments can you make to improve your bubble wand? List them and sketch the changes you want to make.

_____

_____

SHARE: Describe the results of your project. _____

_____

_____

Do you think your design would be a good one to sell in stores?   **YES   NO**

Why or why not? _____

_____

SURFACE TENSION

> **5 sessions:** 1 session for each activity (approximately 1 to $1\frac{1}{2}$ hours per session)

Focus: **Physical Science**—properties of water
Chemistry—atoms and molecules

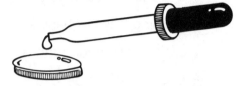

CONNECTIONS AND SUGGESTIONS

SCIENCE—Students will use the scientific method to learn about water molecules. Molecules of water are strongly attracted to each other. This is referred to as *cohesion*. It is evident at any level of water. At the top of a layer of water, water molecules join together with even stronger bonds. They form a rounded shape called a *meniscus*. The droplets shaped by this cohesion are spherical because they are pulled into the tightest possible shape. Students will explore the nature of a meniscus strong enough to support materials placed on it (paper clips, bugs, paper, etc.). Students will discuss applications for using surface tension, such as allowing boats to float, and explore breaking surface tension. Soap and alcohol are two materials that break surface tension because the molecules in them are different and less cohesive.

TECHNOLOGY—Students can use computers or personal tablets to do research on water molecules and surface tension. Additionally, they can photograph or record their observations and document the results of their explorations.

ENGINEERING—Students may use the design process to find ways to more accurately drip water droplets from droppers in order to create meniscuses on coins. They will experiment to devise methods or apparatus that can be used to float objects on a meniscus.

MATH—Students will create graphs and charts in order to illustrate meniscus information. Students will use a variety of mathematic concepts and applications to compare and evaluate the success of science and engineering strategies related to surface tension.

> **DISCUSSION PROMPT:** What is surface tension, and why is it important?
>
> A *surface* is the top or outer layer of something. Let's all look around and identify some surfaces—top of desks or shelves, a part of a pencil you hold, or your skin. *Tension* can mean to be stretched tight. When we talk about the *surface tension* of water, we are referring to the tendency of water molecules to stick together (*bond*) more tightly at the surface of water than they do below the surface.
>
> The *cohesion* of water molecules to create surface tension on water is vital to everyday life. These concepts apply to many aspects of science. These involve things as simple as the tendency of leaves and light, flat objects to float on water and the ability of humans to float on and swim in water. Applications are seen in many instances. A diver landing in a belly flop can feel the sting of these two water features. A small boat uses surface tension and cohesion to remain buoyant. Boats, ships, swimming gear, and anything else related to holding, moving, or using quantities of water are based on the tendency of molecules to adhere to each other and the special strength of the bond at the surface of water. There are over a million molecules in a single drop of water. That is a lot of attraction!

SURFACE TENSION

UNIT MATERIALS (for a class of 30 to 35)

- ☐ 3–8 oz. plastic cups
- ☐ bussing trays or basins
- ☐ carbonated soda (drink)
- ☐ clear plastic cups
- ☐ coins—pennies, nickels, dimes, quarters
- ☐ cooking oil
- ☐ cotton swabs
- ☐ dried herbs
- ☐ eyedroppers or pipettes
- ☐ hair conditioner

- ☐ index cards
- ☐ liquid food coloring
- ☐ liquid dish soap
- ☐ liquid hand soap
- ☐ measuring cups
- ☐ paper clips, small and large
- ☐ paper towels
- ☐ plastic lids or trays
- ☐ rubbing alcohol
- ☐ rulers

- ☐ scissors
- ☐ shampoo
- ☐ slivers of bar soap
- ☐ small Styrofoam™ trays or plates
- ☐ thin straws
- ☐ vinegar
- ☐ water
- ☐ waxed paper

Note: Any small plastic or paper cup will do, but small portion cups like the kinds found in restaurants for condiments or salsas seem to be the most economical.

FIND OUT MORE

Atoms and Molecules-Basic Animation Lessons for Kids
(Teacher Note: Use the first three minutes of this video.)
https://www.youtube.com/watch?v=vlSOESXQI7o

How Molecules Are Formed
https://www.youtube.com/watch?v=lOXxFaHbIXg

Make Me Genius—States of Matter-Episode 1
http://www.makemegenius.com/learn_video.php?id=41&p=25&g=5

Penny Ante (Surface Tension)
A visual of drops being added to a penny to create a meniscus
https://www.youtube.com/watch?v=pvkcP1cacvQ

Science for kids—Soap boat water experiment
Experiments for surface tension and boat races. (Note: Presenter uses oregano instead of pepper.)
https://www.youtube.com/watch?v=qz9hkWhZfRM

Surface Tension: The Pepper Scatter Experiment
https://www.youtube.com/watch?v=0nx19B7TD0Q

Water—To Stick or Not to Stick
Properties of cohesion, adhesion, and surface tension
https://www.youtube.com/watch?v=CT4pURpXkbY

Safety Note: All websites should be checked prior to student viewing to be certain that content is appropriate.

SURFACE TENSION VOCABULARY

<u>accurate</u>—exact, correct in the details

<u>apparatus</u>—scientific equipment

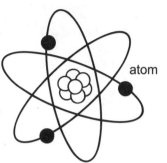
atom

<u>atom</u>—the basic building block of matter which makes up everything on Earth: the smallest particle of an element that has all the characteristics of the element.

<u>bond</u>—ability of two objects to stick together

<u>buoyant</u>—able to float because of width, density, and/or shape

<u>cohesive</u>—two similar things that are attracted to each other or stick to each other
Example: the tendency of water molecules to stick to each other

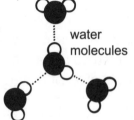
water
molecules

<u>data</u>—facts or information used to analyze or plan something

<u>matter</u>— any object that occupies space and has weight. Matter is found in three states—solid, liquid, and gas.
Examples: ice, water, steam (water vapor)

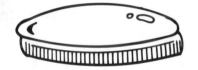

<u>meniscus</u>—the surface of a column of water where cohesion of molecules is strongest

<u>molecule</u>—two or more atoms join together; atom + atom = molecule

<u>notch</u>—a V or U shaped cut

<u>sliver</u>—a thin piece of wood, soap, or other material

<u>surface</u>—an outside layer or part of something

<u>tension</u>—stretched tight

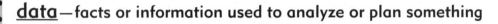

<u>surface tension</u>—the tendency of molecules of water to bond more tightly at the surface of water. The sticking together of the molecules on the surface of a liquid allows it to behave like an elastic skin. This "skin" is what allows leaves to float on water and insects to appear to "walk on water."

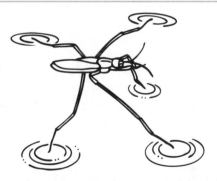

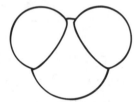

SURFACE TENSION

MOLECULES

Everything around us is made of matter. Everything we see is a solid, a liquid, or a gas. An atom is the basic building block of all matter. Atoms are too small to see. One pencil dot can have billions of atoms on it. That's right—billions!

If two tiny atoms join together, they can form a molecule. You cannot see a molecule either. Scientists study molecules using very special machines. An electron microscope is one tool they use. Using these tools helps us learn what makes different forms of matter—such as water.

Each water molecule is made up of two hydrogen molecules and one oxygen molecule. They form a V shape. Water molecules stick to each other very well. They are called *cohesive* molecules because they can stick together. There are about 1.7 septillion molecules in a single drop of water! It takes trillions and trillions of molecules to make a human body.

1. Look at the model of a water molecule. Scientists say it forms a **V**.
   Use a pencil to draw the **V** on the model.
   Color the oxygen molecule blue.
   Color the hydrogen molecules red.

2. The number 1.7 septillion has 23 zeros. Add the zeros to complete the number.

   1,7_____

3. H_2O is a way to describe the molecule for water. Can you see why? Explain.

   _____

   _____

4. What vocabulary word could be used instead of the word "tool"? _____

5. Draw two or three cohesive water molecules. Remember, if the molecules are cohesive, they are stuck together.

SURFACE TENSION

WATER-DROP RACE

Have water-drop races. If possible, do this activity outside. The goal is to see who can get his or her water drop across the table the fastest.

> **MATERIALS**
> * straws
> * towels
> * water
> * waxed paper

Directions

1. Lay a long sheet of waxed paper along the long end of a table or the floor. Have paper towels or cloth towels nearby.

2. Choose a person to be the observer. This person will yell "**START**" and then watch to see who the winner is.

3. Each student will use an eyedropper or pipette to put one drop of water on the wax paper.

4. Examine your water drop. Do all the drops look similar to your drop?   **YES   NO**

   Explain. _____

5. Each student will use a straw to blow his or her water drop along the length of the waxed paper.

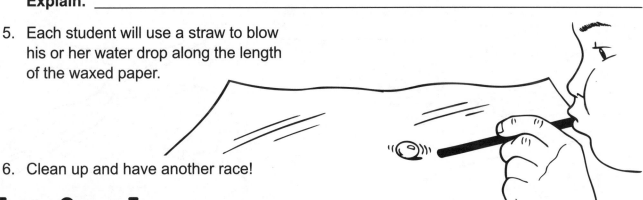

6. Clean up and have another race!

THINK ABOUT IT

1. Circle three words that best describe your water drop. Use the words in a descriptive sentence or write one using your own descriptive words.

BUBBLE	DOME-SHAPED	JIGGLING	SEE-THROUGH
CLEAR	FLAT	SMOOTH	SEMI-CIRCLE

   _____

   _____

2. How does it feel to blow millions of water molecules in one drop across the paper with a tiny straw?

   _____

3. Why do you think the wax paper works so well? _____

   _____

SURFACE TENSION

SURFACE TENSION ON THE LAKE

Today, our friend Nancy is taking us on a hike around the lake to find examples of surface tension. I learned that things can float on water because of surface tension, but I have never gone looking for examples. Nancy is a scientist. She says there are many interesting examples once you know what to look for.

We go early in the morning when the dew is still on the leaves. Those water drops resting on the leaves are our first example! When we tilt a leaf, the dew drops run together and form a larger drop. We look closely and see the *meniscus*. That is the rounded surface of the drop.

Next, we go down to the edge of the lake. There are leaves floating on the water. Nancy explains that the water molecules stick together and hold things up. This is called *surface tension*. We look around and see other floating items—a bug, a boat, and a little yellow ball. The surface tension of the water helps them all float.

Directions: Look at the lake scene below. Circle five items showing surface tension that were mentioned in the passage above.

Observe: Gather droppers, a variety of leaves, paper towels, and cups of water. Work outside if possible.

1. Take turns adding drops of water to different leaves.
2. Did all the leaves you gathered hold drops of water?   **YES   NO**
3. Discuss your observations.

COIN MENISCUS

Teacher Preparation: Divide the students into small groups for the coin meniscus activities. If time is short, each group can work with a different coin—*pennies, nickels, dimes,* or *quarters*.

Each student will have a turn to count the number of drops he or she can add to a dry coin before the water overflows. Team members will record their individual counts on the chart on page 111. Later, counts for all coins will be evaluated by the class.

Note: Before beginning the unit activities, allow time for students to practice using the pipettes or eyedroppers. It takes a while to become adept at slowly making one drop at a time come out of the dropper.

TEAM MATERIALS

- 4 oz. of water for each student
- cloth or paper towels
- copy of *How Many Drops Fit on a _____?*
- cups or containers
- eyedroppers or plastic pipettes
- measuring cups
- plastic lids or trays
- dimes
- nickels
- quarters
- pennies
- camera (optional)

DROPPER PRACTICE

To do the activities in this unit students need to be able to control the number of drops that come out of an eyedropper or pipette. Allow time to practice using the tools. Take turns.

1. To begin, set up a work area with a tray or lid, some water, and droppers. Squeeze some of the air out of the dropper in order to let water in. Squeeze water in and out of the pipette or eyedropper.

2. Try making streams of water by pinching the bulb and squeezing all the water out of the tube at the same time.

3. Try making individual drops. Practice until you can make 10 individual drops.

4. Is it more difficult to make a stream of water or an individual drop?

   Explain. _____

   _____

5. See which method works better, filling the dropper with water up to the bulb or leaving room at the top of the tube.

   Explain your choice. _____

   _____

   _____

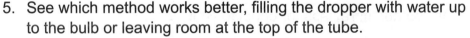

COIN MENISCUS

Directions: Read all the steps before beginning this activity. Notice where you will be counting and when you should be taking pictures.

COIN MENISCUS—SET UP

1. Each student should have a coin, a plastic lid, water, a dropper or pipette, and a dry cloth or paper towel. Try to have a camera ready to photograph the meniscus.
2. Arrange the dry coin on the plastic lid. Fill each cup with 4 oz. of water.
3. Set up the water cups so each team member can reach them easily.
4. Test your pipette or dropper to make certain it is working well.
5. Dry the coin and prepare to begin.

COIN MENISCUS—HOW MANY DROPS!

1. Which coin will your team be testing? _____

   Question: How many drops of water do you think this coin will hold before spilling over?

   Hypothesis: _____

   _____

2. Make certain everyone is seated and be careful not to bump the table or each other.
3. Use an eyedropper or pipette to place one drop of water on the head side of your **dry** coin.
4. Examine the shape of the drop. Observe the meniscus. Describe the meniscus.

   _____

   _____

5. Carefully add more drops of water, one at a time. Go slowly. Place as many drops as you can on the head of the coin. Do you notice a change in the shape of the meniscus?

   YES   NO

6. Draw what you observed in the sketch space. Try to be accurate. Is the top rounded, or are the sides rounded but the top flat? Does it have a different shape?
7. Keep an accurate count of drops until the meniscus breaks.
8. How many drops did you get on your first try? _____

   Was the number of drops you got more, less, or equal to your hypothesis?

   MORE   LESS   EQUAL TO

9. Dry the coin, flip it over, and do the same test on the tails side.

   How many drops did the tails side hold? _____

   Which side held more drops?   **HEADS   TAILS**

COIN MENISCUS

Directions

1. Fill in the name of the coin your team will use in the blank at the top of the chart below.

   Note: If you prefer, recreate this chart on your tablet or computer. See page 42 for basic directions.

2. Fill in the number of drops on the coin in the second column.

3. Write your initials next to your number of drops in the Tester column.

4. Continue until all team members have added drops to their coins and filled in the chart. Add more rows to the chart if necessary. Use the back of the page.

HOW MANY DROPS FIT ON A _____?		
COIN	NUMBER OF DROPS	TESTER
Coin 1		
Coin 2		
Coin 3		
Coin 4		
Coin 5		
Coin 6		

ANALYZE THE DATA—LOOK AT THE MATH

1. What was the greatest number of drops on the coin? _____

2. What was the smallest number of drops on the coin? _____

3. Find the *difference* between the largest and the smallest number of drops. _____

4. Find the *average number of drops* for the coin. _____

COIN MENISCUS

DATA REVIEW

Analyze the class data and share your observations. Display the charts for all the coins so that all classmates can see them. Arrange them in order beginning with the penny chart on the left and ending with the one for quarters on the right.

1. What is the first thing you notice about the data for the different coins?

   _____

   _____

2. Which coin held the most drops? _____

   Why do you think this coin held the most? _____

   _____

   _____

3. What can you determine after analyzing the data on the charts? _____

   _____

   _____

4. **Troubleshoot:** What are the main problems you encountered, and how might you solve these problems?

   _____

   _____

   _____

   _____

5. Do you think some trials should be redone?   **YES**   **NO**

   Why or why not? _____

   _____

   Describe what you would do. _____

   _____

   _____

 _____

COIN MENISCUS

JOURNAL ENTRY

1. What did you learn about working with droppers?

   _____

   _____

   _____

2. Explain what causes a meniscus to "bubble" above the coin.

   _____

   _____

   _____

3. What actions caused the meniscus to overflow?

   _____

   _____

   _____

4. What surprised you most about the meniscuses on the coins?

   _____

   _____

   _____

5. Have you noticed a meniscus somewhere since doing your experiments? If so, describe it.

   _____

   _____

   _____

SCIENTIFIC METHOD REVIEW—COIN MENISCUS

Directions: Share your observations, journal entries, and other documentation about your work creating meniscuses on coins in a discussion led by your teacher.

CUP MENISCUS

Directions: Read ALL the steps before beginning this activity. Notice where you will be counting drops and when you should be documenting the activity and/or taking pictures. Keep in mind that working with drops of water requires slow, careful movements.

TEAM MATERIALS

- 2–4 oz. plastic cups
- camera or tablet (optional)
- eyedroppers or pipettes
- paper towels
- rulers
- water

NOTE: Any small plastic or paper cup will work but small portion cups like the kinds found in restaurants for condiments or salsa seem to be the most economical (and easiest to fill quickly).

Directions

1. Fill the small cup with water up to $\frac{1}{2}$ centimeter from the top of the cup.

    Question: How many drops of water do you think you can add to this cup before it spills over?

    Write your estimate as a hypothesis.

    Hypothesis: _____

    _____

    _____

2. Use a dropper to fill the cup with water. Try to get the water level as close to the top of the cup as possible.

3. Begin counting the drops. Slowly add more drops of water until the cup is actually overfull. Go slow. You do not want the water to spill over!

4. Stop when you can see that the meniscus is getting large.

5. Write down the number of drops you have added so far, so that you do not forget them.

NUMBER OF DROPS

Observation: What happens if you touch the tip of the dropper to a meniscus?

_____

_____

_____

_____

CUP MENISCUS

Directions *(cont.)*

6. Take a picture of the meniscus or draw it in the cup to the right.

   Note: If the meniscus already overflowed, fill the cup and start counting drops again.

7. Continue filling the cup carefully and counting the drops of water until the meniscus overflows.

   How many drops did it take altogether before it overflowed? Don't forget to add in the drops from #5.

   NUMBER OF DROPS: _____ + _____ = _____

8. Clean up the spilled water and prepare to carry out additional trials.

CHARTING YOUR RESULTS

Directions: Use chart making instructions from page 42 or page 59 to create a chart or use the one below that can record and compare your information.

CUP MENISCUS		
TRIAL	# OF DROPS	CAUSE OF SPILL
First		
Second		
Third		
Fourth		
Fifth		

CUP MENISCUS

JOURNAL ENTRY

1. What strategy did you use to add drops to the meniscus?

    _____

    _____

    _____

2. Have you seen a meniscus at home, at school, or in any other setting? If so, where?

    _____

    _____

3. How is this activity related to the "drops on a coin" in the last activity?

    _____

    _____

    _____

4. Were the meniscuses in the two activities similar or different? _____

    Explain. _____

    _____

5. Draw examples of your coin and cup meniscuses.

SCIENTIFIC METHOD REVIEW—CUP MENISCUS

Directions: Gather with your teacher and classmates. Take turns sharing your observations, journal entries, and other documentation about your work creating meniscuses on small cups of water.

 _____

MOVING BOATS

Teacher Preparation: Partners will need to share large water containers and will need to take turns testing their boats.

TEAM MATERIALS

- bus trays, tubs, or a small plastic wading pool
- clear cups or containers of various sizes
- cooking oil
- eyedroppers or pipettes
- rubbing alcohol
- rulers—standard and metric

- thin Styrofoam™ plates, trays, and/or cups
- liquid hand soap, liquid dish soap, or shampoo
- scissors
- slivers of bar soap

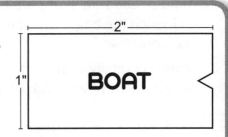

SOAP-POWERED BOATS—SET UP

1. Fill a large container with water.
2. Cut small pieces of Styrofoam™ into rectangles 2" long and 1" wide. Try to be precise.
3. Cut a small notch on one end (back) and shape the front end like a boat. Use the example in the Materials box above as a guide.
4. Trace your boat in the sketch box.

MOVING SOAP-POWERED BOATS

1. Place a small Styrofoam™ boat on the water that is in the container.
2. Squeeze the rubber end of a dropper gently to put one drop of liquid soap in the notch at the back of the boat.
3. What happens when the liquid soap is added to the back of the boat?

_____

4. Use a ruler to measure or estimate the distance your boat moved.

   How far did the boat move? _____

5. Do two more trials and record your results below.

	SOAP-POWERED BOATS	
TRIAL	**WHAT DIRECTION DOES THE BOAT MOVE?**	**HOW FAR DOES THE BOAT MOVE?**
1		
2		
3		

6. Analyze the data. What was the farthest distance your soap boat moved on one drop of liquid soap? _____

NAME _____

MOVING BOATS

SOAP-POWERED BOAT RACES—TRIAL 1

1. Hold a race with your partner. Use one drop of liquid soap to launch the boats simultaneously from the same end of the container.

2. Watch carefully to see where each boat stops. Think of a way to mark where each boat stops. Describe what you did.

_____

_____

3. Do at least two trial races. Try to measure the distance each time using a ruler.

4. Fill in each partner's name at the top of the chart. Record the results in centimeters.

NAME		
1ST TRIAL	CM	CM
2ND TRIAL	CM	CM
3RD TRIAL	CM	CM

5. Analyze the data. Whose boat went farther on one drop of liquid soap? _____

   Why do you think this happened? _____

_____

SOAP-POWERED BOAT RACES—TRIAL 2

1. Make another boat. This model should be at least 3 cm longer.

2. Make a notch or two in the back to place the drop of liquid soap.

3. Describe the changes you made to the new boat.

_____

_____

4. Did it go faster or farther? _____

   Describe your results. _____

_____

 **NAME** _____

MOVING BOATS

RUBBING ALCOHOL-POWERED BOATS—SET UP

1. Fill a large container with water.

2. Prepare clean droppers and small cups of rubbing alcohol.

3. Use the boats from the soap-powered boats lesson or create new ones using Styrofoam™ trays or plates.

4. Describe the boat you will use. _____

_____

TESTING RUBBING ALCOHOL-POWERED BOATS

1. Place your boat on the water.

2. Squeeze the rubber end of a dropper gently to put one drop of rubbing alcohol in the notch at the back of the boat.

3. What happens when the rubbing alcohol is added to the back of the boat? _____

_____

4. Use a ruler to measure how far you observed your boat move.

   How far did the boat move? _____

5. Do three more trials and record your results below.

TRIAL	WHAT HAPPENS WHEN ALCOHOL IS ADDED	HOW FAR DOES THE BOAT GO?
1		
2		
3		

6. Analyze the data. What was the farthest distance your alcohol-powered boat moved on one drop of alcohol?

_____

VARIATIONS

—Add a full dropper of oil to the water. What happens to your boat when you try to move it with soap or alcohol on the oily water?

—Try wedging a small sliver of hand soap in a small notch at the rear of a small Styrofoam™ boat. Describe what happens.

MOVING BOATS

JOURNAL ENTRY

1. Describe what you learned about the surface tension of water from this experiment.

_____

_____

_____

2. How did liquid soap affect the movement of the boat?

_____

_____

_____

3. How did rubbing alcohol affect the movement of the boat?

_____

_____

_____

4. Explain why breaking the surface tension of the water allows the boats to move.

_____

_____

_____

5. Describe other variations you tried.

_____

_____

_____

SCIENTIFIC METHOD REVIEW—MOVING BOATS

Directions: Share your observations, journal entries, and other documentation about your work creating and racing boats. Explain what you learned about surface tension and moving objects in a discussion led by your teacher.

 _____

FLOATING CLIPS

Teacher Preparation: This activity will involve spilled water. If possible do this activity outside or place absorbent towels under the water tubs and have paper towels available.

TEAM MATERIALS

- 6-ounce clear plastic cups
- eyedroppers or pipettes
- index cards
- large paper clips
- small paper clips
- paper
- paper towels
- toothpicks
- water
- water tubs

Directions: Work in pairs. Share materials.

FLOATING SMALL PAPER CLIPS

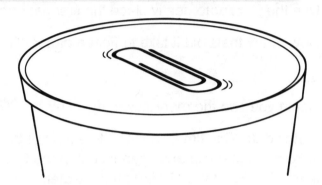

1. Place a towel or paper towels under a cup. Fill the cup with water to just below the rim.

2. Try to float a small paper clip on the water. You may need to try more than once.

3. Were you successful?   **YES**   **NO**

   Explain what worked or what the problem was. _____

   _____

   _____

4. Now add a bit more water to the cup to create a meniscus.

   Can you see the meniscus?   **YES**   **NO**

   If no, carefully add more water until the meniscus is visible.

5. Draw the meniscus on the cup in the sketchbox.

6. Try to float the paper clip again. Give it a few tries.

   Were you successful?   **YES**   **NO**

7. Explain what worked or what the problem was. _____

   _____

   _____

8. Add the paper clip to your drawing.

FLOATING CLIPS

WHICH APPROACH WORKS BEST?

Method 1: Use the fingernail tips of your thumb and forefinger to gently place a small paper clip on the surface of the water.

How many tries did it take to get the clip to float? _____

Could you see the meniscus in the clip?   **YES   NO**

Method 2: Get the second small paper clip and bend it into an "**L** shape." Use the "**L**-clip" to gently place the first paper clip on the water.

How many trials did it take to float a paper clip using an "**L**-clip?"

_____

Could you see the meniscus in the clip?   **YES   NO**

Method 3: This time, change the shape of the clip you want to float. Take the paper clip and open it so that the two loops look like a long letter "**S**." Float the "**S**-clip" on the water.

Could you see the meniscus in each half loop of the paper clip?

YES   NO

How many trials did it take to float the **S**-shaped paper clip? _____

1. Which method worked best for you to float the small paper clips?

    FINGERTIPS   FINGERNAILS   L-CLIP   S-SHAPED CLIP

    Why? _____

    _____

2. Take a class poll to see how many students preferred each method. Use tally marks to show the results in the chart below. Discuss.

    _____

FINGERTIPS	FINGERNAILS	L-CLIP	S-CLIP

FLOATING CLIPS

Teacher Preparation: In the last activity, students attempted to float small paper clips in water. In this activity, they will try to float larger paper clips using support materials that will serve as rafts or boats. Introduce the new materials (paper towel squares, toothpicks, index cards, paper) and arrange them in the testing area before students begin.

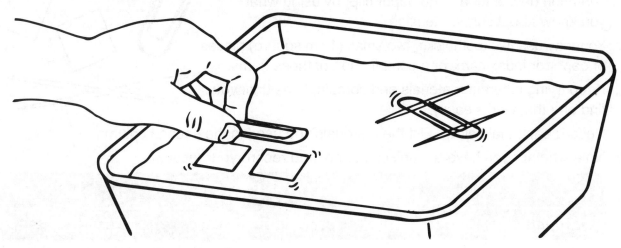

FLOATING LARGE PAPER CLIPS

1. Try floating a large paper clip. Make at least three attempts. You may need to adjust your water levels and to check the meniscus.

2. Use any of the methods from the previous activity or try something new.

   Once you have suceeded in floating a clip, describe what worked. _____

   _____

   _____

   If no method worked, describe the ways you tried to float the large clip. _____

   _____

   _____

3. Do you have an idea for another way to try? If yes, explain. _____

   _____

   _____

NAME

FLOATING CLIPS

FLOATATION AIDS

1. Think about the different methods you tried in order to float a small paper clip. This time you will create a floatation device for a large paper clip, by using what you know about surface tension.

2. You may use two toothpicks, two small (1 cm square) pieces of paper or index card, or a combination of those items.

3. Keep trying different materials and combinations until you find one that works easily.

4. Record each trial below. List the materials you used in the second column.

5. Note whether you have a meniscus or not and record your results.

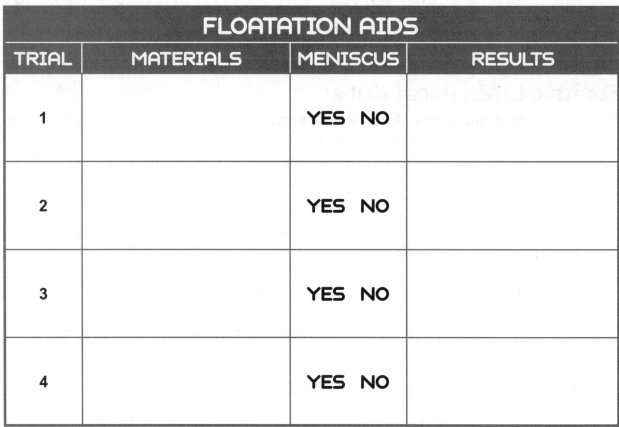

FLOATATION AIDS			
TRIAL	MATERIALS	MENISCUS	RESULTS
1		YES NO	
2		YES NO	
3		YES NO	
4		YES NO	

ANALYZE THE DATA

How many trials did it take to float a large paper clip? _____

Could you see the meniscus in the loop of the large paper clip?   YES   NO

Why do you think the large paper clip is hard to float? _____

_____

ⓃⓐⓂⓔ _____

FLOATING CLIPS

JOURNAL ENTRY

1. Was it easier to float small or large paper clips on water? Explain.

_____

_____

_____

2. Did it matter if you had a meniscus or not? Explain.

_____

_____

_____

3. What have you learned about surface tension?

_____

_____

_____

4. Did you do any extra research on this activity? If so, describe what you learned or tried to do.

_____

_____

_____

5. Is there another way to float a paper clip that you would like to try? Explain.

_____

_____

_____

SCIENTIFIC METHOD REVIEW—FLOATING CLIPS

Directions: Explain what you learned about surface tension and floating objects. Share your observations, journal entries, and other documentation about your attempts to float paper clips in a discussion led by your teacher.

CHALLENGE: BE A CHEMIST—FIND THE FASTEST FUEL

Teacher Preparation: Gather the "fuel" options and other materials needed. Arrange areas for testing the fuels and for racing the boats. Have students work in pairs using the Scientific Method. If appropriate, have students watch the surface tension videos suggested on page 104.

"FUEL" OPTIONS
- cooking oil
- dish soap
- food coloring
- hair conditioner
- hand soap
- rubbing alcohol
- shampoo
- soda (carbonated drink)
- vinegar

OTHER MATERIALS
- bus trays, cookie sheets, or a small plastic wading pool
- cotton swabs
- eyedroppers or pipettes
- ice cube trays
- dried parsley or black pepper
- scissors
- small cups or lids
- small plates
- rulers
- thin Styrofoam™ trays or plates

CHALLENGE: Work in pairs to test a variety of liquids. Find the best liquid to break the surface tension. Use what you know about water molecules and surface tension. Later you will make boats and race them using the chosen "fuels."

QUESTION: Discuss the choices with your partner. Choose one question to test.

☐ Which liquid will break the surface tension and make the boat move the fastest?

☐ Which liquid will break the surface tension and make the boat move the farthest?

RESEARCH: Test the ability of different "fuel" options to break the surface tension of water.

1. List the three fuels you will test.

    ①_____ ②_____ ③_____

2. Fill a small round plate with water. Sprinkle in about a teaspoon of parsley or pepper.
3. Fill cups or lids with small amounts of the "fuel" options to be tested.
4. Dip your finger or a cotton swab into each fuel and then into the center of the parsley or pepper to test each liquid. Does it break the surface tension?

5. After each test, record your findings on the chart on the next page.

WHAT IS YOUR HYPOTHESIS?:

Describe which fuel you think will work the best to answer the question above that you have chosen to test.

_____

_____

 _____

CHALLENGE: BE A CHEMIST—FIND THE FASTEST FUEL

TEST YOUR HYPOTHESIS:

Describe the reaction of each "fuel" tested in the chart below.

FUEL	REACTION

ANALYZE: Did you succeed in proving your hypothesis?   **YES**   **NO**

Explain. _____

_____

_____

TROUBLESHOOT: If you could do the testing over, would you do anything differently?

YES   NO   If so, what would you do differently and why? _____

_____

_____

_____

CHALLENGE: BE A CHEMIST—FIND THE FASTEST FUEL

TEST: Demonstrate your findings by racing the boats using the "fuel" you found worked best to break the surface tension.

1. Each teammate will make a Styrofoam™ boat to test their fuel choice. Cut a boat that is 2" long and 1" wide.

   Make one or more notches in the back and curve the front to resemble a boat.

   Trace your boat in the frame on the right.

2. Arrange the boats at one end of a tray or small pool. Each racer should have a cotton swab with his/her chosen fuel ready.

3. Choose a person to yell "**START**" and observe the race. (This person will have a turn to race later.)

4. Take turns placing fuel in a notch in the back of a boat to race.

5. Race until all students have had turns.

COMMUNICATE RESULTS:

Did you succeed in proving your hypothesis?   **YES   NO**

Explain. _____

_____

Do you think the testing process for fuels and the surface tension using the dry, flaky herbs was useful?

YES   NO

Explain. _____

_____

What surprised you the most about your study of surface tension? Share your thoughts.

_____

_____

THE POWER OF WIND

> **5 sessions:** 1 session for each activity (approximately 1 to $1\frac{1}{2}$ hours per session)

Focus: Physical Science—properties of wind

CONNECTIONS AND SUGGESTIONS

SCIENCE—Most students experience winds of various speeds in the normal course of a year. The activities in this unit would normally be done during windy days, but they will also work with fans, if needed. Students will use the Design Method to create "machines" to observe the behavior of moving air, or wind. They will spend time determining wind direction, observing and comparing wind speed, and using wind with tools and toys.

TECHNOLOGY—Students can use computers or personal tablets to research the power of wind and learn more about wind measurement tools. Additionally they can photograph or record their observations and/or document the results of their explorations of wind power using video.

ENGINEERING—Most students will be working with light or moderate winds. The weather vanes, anemometers, pinwheels, and wind wheels built in this unit are designed to give visual comparisons of wind speeds. Students may also use the design process to adjust their wind speed indicators for more efficiency and to find ways to use the force of wind to do work. If time allows they will make size adjustments on shapes on the weather vanes and cup sizes on the anemometers.

MATH—Students will use standard measurements and metric measurements to create a variety of wind devices. They will follow guidelines to make geometric shapes with specific dimensions. They will use graphs and charts to track wind direction and speed or force. They will also make time comparisons.

DISCUSSION PROMPT: What Is Wind?

The movement of the air is what we call wind. The sun's uneven heating of Earth causes wind. All you need is two areas of different pressure. They can be caused by water, cloud cover, mountains, etc. Here is how it works:

1. The sun radiates energy and shines on Earth. This energy heats the land and water.

2. The air over the land gets warmer and expands. It becomes less dense.

3. The warm air rises over the land.

4. Then, cooler air over water moves inland and pushes the warm air up higher.

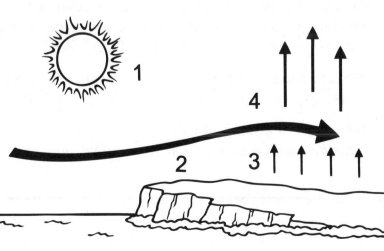

THE POWER OF WIND

UNIT MATERIALS (for a class of 30 to 35)

- ☐ 6–8 oz. paper cups
- ☐ 12 oz. paper cups
- ☐ cellophane tape
- ☐ compasses
- ☐ construction paper
- ☐ drinking straws
- ☐ electric fans or hair dryers*
- ☐ hole punches or large nails
- ☐ manila folders
- ☐ markers

- ☐ masking tape
- ☐ modeling clay
- ☐ plastic water bottles with caps
- ☐ pushpins
- ☐ rulers
- ☐ scissors
- ☐ timers or stopwatches
- ☐ unsharpened pencils
- ☐ water
- ☐ wooden barbeque skewers

* If you can count on the wind blowing, you will not need the fans or hair dryers.

FIND OUT MORE

Bill Nye the Science Guy on Wind
https://www.youtube.com/watch?v=uBqohRu2RRk

What Makes Wind? *The KidsKnowIt* **Network**
Provides explanation and an example of a demonstration (with adult supervision) of high and low pressure. The demonstration uses ice, a lamp, smoke, and an aquarium.
https://www.youtube.com/watch?v=D52rTzibFRc

What Is Wind? *SciShow* (View for teacher information)
https://www.youtube.com/watch?v=RzSqhrn2dDM

Why Does the Wind Blow?
https://www.youtube.com/watch?v=xCLwbqmacck

Safety Note: All websites should be checked prior to student viewing to be certain that content is appropriate.

THE POWER OF WIND VOCABULARY

air—a gas that we breathe

anemometer—a device for measuring and comparing wind speed

modification—adjustment, change

pinwheel—a child's toy for watching the effects of moving air

pointer—the part of a weather vane that shows the direction from which the wind is coming

weather vane—also known as a wind vane; it is an instrument, usually placed on top of a house, which shows the direction the wind is blowing

rotation—move or cause to move in a circle around an axis or center

windsock—a cone-like tube used to tell the direction and speed of the wind; often found at airports

wind—air that moves—usually in a horizontal motion

BEAUFORT WIND SCALE

The *Beaufort Wind Scale* is used to measure the speed of wind on a scale of 1 to 12.

  0 CALM—no noticeable wind

 1–3 LIGHT WIND—leaves and twigs on a tree or the ground move; flags blow

 4–5 MODERATE WIND—produces waves on a pool or lake; thin trees move

 6–7 STRONG WIND—large trees sway; leaves often fall; walking can be difficult for adults

 8–9 GALE—damage to roofs and trees

10–11 STORM—serious damage to buildings

  12 HURRICANE—massive destruction (speeds over 73 miles per hour)

1. Which is the strongest wind level you have experienced? _____

2. Describe what you observed. _____

_____

THE POWER OF WIND

WHO KNEW?

WIND

WIND

Wind occurs when the air outside moves or flows. As long as the sun shines, there will be wind. Earth heating up and cooling down causes the movement we call wind.

Wind can be helpful. Long ago, windmills were used to grind wheat or corn. They also pumped water and ran sawmills that produced wood for builders.

A light wind, or breeze, can keep us cool on hot days. It can dry clothes hanging on a line or blow fall leaves around the yard. Wind blows sailboats across the water and lifts planes and blimps in the air. Wind is clean energy and it is renewable. It makes wind turbines on wind farms move. The energy from the wind turbines makes electricity.

Often, seeds from plants and flowers are picked up by the wind and carried to other places. This can be a good thing since it spreads plants. It can be a problem if the seeds are weeds or other plants people do not want on their land.

Wind can cause problems if it gets too strong. Heavy winds can cause damage to trees and buildings. Cold or freezing winds can damage crops. Hurricanes are very strong winds and can be quite destructive. They can cause serious damage to communities.

1. When is the wind helpful? _____

_____

_____

2. When is the wind destructive? _____

_____

_____

3. Name three things you have seen the wind move.

_____

_____

_____

WIND DIRECTION

Teacher Preparation: Provide books and websites to allow students to do some research on weather vanes before beginning the activity. Explain that a weather vane is a simple way to determine the direction of the wind or moving air. A weather vane points in the direction the wind is moving. Be prepared to use electric fans or hair dryers if there is no wind to test weather vanes. Testing takes place over five days.

TEAM MATERIALS

- 12 oz. paper cup
- cellophane tape
- directional compass
- electric fans or hairdryers
- heavy paper—tag board, index cards, or manila folders
- masking tape

- markers
- modeling clay
- pushpins and straight pins
- rulers
- scissors
- straight straws—regular or wide-mouthed
- unsharpened pencils with good erasers

Directions: Use the directions below to make a weather vane. Work in teams of two.

MAKING A WEATHER VANE

1. Use heavy paper to make a circle that is 2" in diameter or use the pattern on this page.

2. Draw an equilateral triangle on heavy paper. Each side should be 2" long. Use the triangle on this page as a guide or a pattern. The triangle will be the "pointer" for the weather vane.

3. Cut a plastic straight straw so that it is 7" long. The straw will hold the triangle (pointer) and the circle.

4. Use a ruler to measure 1" in from each end of the straw. Mark these 1" points by drawing a circle around the straw at each point marked.

5. Carefully press the end of the straw together to cut it and create slits on the top and bottom. Cut from the end of the straw to the 1" line. Do this on both ends.

6. Slide the 2" circle into the straw slit on one end. Slide the pointer (triangle) into the straw slit on the other end of the straw.

7. Use tape to keep the circle and pointer in place.

8. Measure exactly half the distance of the straw (the $3\frac{1}{2}$" mark) to find the halfway point.

9. Stick a pushpin or a straight pin through the straw at this point. Make sure the circle and triangle are vertical (straight up and down).

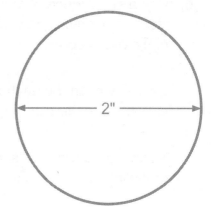

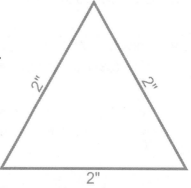

WIND DIRECTION

MAKING THE WEATHER VANE BASE

1. Cut a 4" square piece of heavy paper for the base.

2. Add the letters **N**, **E**, **S**, and **W** to create a compass to show directions. Place the **N** on one corner of the base and the **S** on the opposite corner. Add an **E** on the right side of the **N** and a **W** on the left side of the **N**.

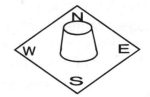

3. Place a sturdy paper cup upside down on the 4" square. Center the cup and draw a circle around it.

4. Find the center of the bottom of the cup (which is now on top). Do this by drawing two straight lines to divide the circle in four equal sections.

5. Use a pushpin to make a small hole at the center where the two lines cross. Wobble the pushpin to make the hole a little bigger. Then take a pencil with a point and make the hole just big enough to hold a new unsharpened pencil.

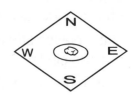

6. Use a small piece of modeling clay about the size of three stacked pennies and stick it on the center of the 4" square piece of tag board.

7. Carefully push the unsharpened pencil through the hole in the cup and into the clay.

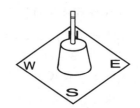

Make sure the pencil is stuck straight up-and-down in the modeling clay. Make sure the cup is on the circle.

8. Use tape to keep the cup in place on the weather vane base.

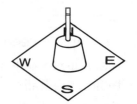

9. Stick the pin through the center of the straw and into the top of the eraser to attach the pointer to the pencil.

10. Twirl the pointer several times to see that it moves freely on the pin. If it doesn't move freely, try a different type of pin.

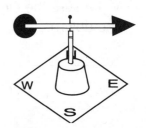

 _____

WIND DIRECTION

USING THE WEATHER VANE

1. Go outside and find a table or other flat area to test your weather vanes.

2. Set the finished weather vane on the flat area.

3. Use a directional compass or have your teacher point out the direction of **North**. Make sure the **N** on the base of your weather vane is facing North.

4. Use masking tape to attach the base of the vane to the flat area.

5. Observe the behavior of the weather vane.

6. Check your weather vane at the beginning (**B**), middle (**M**) and end (**E**) of each day for five days or more.

   Write down the direction each time.

   Use the bottom row of the chart to describe the types of wind that were noticeable each day.

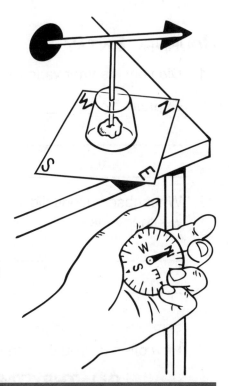

WIND DIRECTION					
DAY	**1**	**2**	**3**	**4**	**5**
DIRECTION	B	B	B	B	B
	M	M	M	M	M
	E	E	E	E	E
STRENGTH					

What is the most common direction from which the wind blows in your area?   **N   S   E   W**

Is there any pattern of wind direction based on the time of day?   **YES   NO**

If so, explain. _____

_____

_____

WIND DIRECTION

JOURNAL ENTRY

1. Did your weather vane work well?   **YES   NO**

    Explain. _____

    _____

    _____

2. What observations did you make about the strength of the wind from the behavior of your weather vane?

    _____

    _____

    _____

3. How often do you think the wind blows in the same direction?

    ALL THE TIME   MOST OF THE TIME   SOMETIMES

    How would you be able to check this? _____

    _____

4. What devices or machines have you noticed that can *make* wind?

    _____   _____   _____

5. What devices have you learned about that can *measure* wind?

    _____   _____   _____

6. What device would you like to make to use the power of moving air, the wind?

    _____

    _____

    _____

DESIGN REVIEW PROCESS—WIND DIRECTION

Share your observations, journal entries, and other documentation about using a weather vane with your classmates in a discussion moderated by your teacher.

(N) (A) (M) (E)

MEASURING WIND SPEED

Teacher Preparation: Share pictures and information about anemometers—instruments for measuring the force or speed of wind. Some are manual and spin around. Explain that older anometers cannot tell the wind speed in miles per hour but can give you an idea of how fast the wind is blowing. Other, more modern ones, are digital and can measure in mph. Determine ahead of time if you will make holes in bottle caps or allow students to do so. (See page 138.)

TEAM MATERIALS

- 1 plastic water bottle with cap
- 1 unsharpened pencil with eraser
- 2 straight, plastic drinking straws
- five 6 oz. paper or plastic cups
- hole punch or nails
- masking tape
- pencils and markers
- rulers

Optional: Be prepared to use electric fans or hair dryers if there is no wind available to test the anemometers during the 5-day activity.

MAKING AN ANEMOMETER

1. Number the cups 1 to 5.

2. Use a pencil to mark a spot about $\frac{3}{4}$" (2 cm) down from the lip of Cups 1, 2, 3, and 4.

3. Use a hole punch or the sharp point of a pencil to make a hole that is just large enough let the plastic straw slide through the opening. Do this for Cups 1–4.

4. Use the hole punch or pencil to make four equally spaced holes around Cup 5. Each hole should be $\frac{3}{4}$" (or 2 cm) down from the lip of the cup.

5. Slide a plastic straw through the hole in Cup 1. Bend the last $\frac{1}{2}$ inch of the straw and tape it to the opposite side of the cup on the inside.

6. Turn the cup on its side and slide the straw through two opposite holes in Cup 5.

7. Push the end of that straw through the hole in Cup 2. Tilt this cup on its side and tape the straw to the inside wall of this cup the same way you did in Cup 1.

8. Use the second straw to connect Cups 3 and 4 in the same way. Once you have attached the straw to Cup 3, push the straw through the remaining two holes in Cup 5. Then connect Cup 4 and secure the straws.

MEASURING WIND SPEED

COMPLETING THE ANEMOMETER

1. Use a pushpin to make a small hole in the bottom of Cup 5. Use the sharp point of a pencil or nail to make that hole just large enough to hold the pencil.
2. Push the pencil through this hole—eraser first—until it reaches the crossed straws at the top of Cup 5.
3. Use the pushpin to attach the two straws to the eraser of the pencil.
4. Fill the water bottle at least half full of water to serve as a heavy base for the anemometer.
5. Make a hole in the plastic bottle cap with the pushpin and sharp point of the pencil. The hole needs to be big enough to allow the pencil to rotate freely.
6. Place the pencil end of the anemometer into the bottle of water.
7. Mark Cup 1 with a large **X** so that you can keep track of the turns.

USING THE ANEMOMETER

1. Spin the anemometer to make sure it moves freely.
2. If possible, place the device on a table in an area away from buildings and trees. Try to place the device where the wind can blow it without obstructions.
3. With your partner, time the number of rotations (turns) in one minute. You can do this by counting the number of times the **X** cup goes past a given point.
4. Do this three times a day throughout the week.
5. Use the chart below to keep the records.

WIND SPEED RECORDS				
NUMBER OF ROTATIONS IN ONE MINUTE				
DAY 1	DAY 2	DAY 3	DAY 4	DAY 5
1st	1st	1st	1st	1st
2nd	2nd	2nd	2nd	2nd
3rd	3rd	3rd	3rd	3rd

EXTENSION—WIND SPEED CALCULATIONS

Calculate the speed of the wind by calculating the number of rotations of your anemometer and multiplying them by the circumference (distance around) of your anemometer. If you followed the directions, this circumference is about 2 feet.

rotations × circumference = wind speed

For example: If you had 40 rotations in one minute, your speed would be 40 times 2 feet or 80 feet per minute.

 NAME _____

MEASURING WIND SPEED

JOURNAL ENTRY

1. Were you able to complete the model anemometer?

    YES   NO

    Sketch your anemometer in the frame on the right.

2. What difficulties did you encounter? _____

    _____

    _____

3. How does the bottle of water help you keep an accurate measure of the wind speed?

    _____

    _____

    _____

4. What would you do to improve the model you made? _____

    _____

    _____

    _____

5. Why do you think it is important to know the speed of the wind?

    _____

    _____

    _____

DESIGN PROCESS REVIEW—MEASURING WIND SPEED

Share your observations, journal entries, and other documentation about your experiences constructing anemometers with your classmates in a discussion led by your teacher.

MAKING PINWHEELS

Teacher Preparation: Share pictures and information about pinwheels—toys that use wind to work. Ask students to share experiences they may have had with pinwheels or places they have seen them.

Be prepared to use electric fans or hair dryers if there is no wind to test the pinwheels.

TEAM MATERIALS

- heavy paper
- large straws or pencils with erasers
- markers
- rulers
- scissors
- straight pins
- tape

Optional: Electric fans or hair dryers if needed due to lack of wind

---

MAKING A SIMPLE PINWHEEL

1. Use a ruler to measure a 6" square on a piece of heavy paper.

2. Cut out the 6" square. Draw two diagonal lines from the corners. The lines should cross, forming four right angles (90°) in the center of the paper.

3. Use the sample below as a guide when labeling the corners of the square. Each triangle should have the letter placed in the same angle. Label the first corner **W**, and continue with **X**, **Y**, and **Z**.

4. Use a ruler to measure 3" from the outer corners along each line.

5. Cut along each line to the 3" point.

6. Pull corner **W** down to the middle of the paper and tape it to form a loop. Then pull corner **X** down and tape it. Do the same with corners **Y** and **Z**. Do not fold the corners.

7. Push a straight pin through all the taped corners in the center of the model wheel and then stick the pin into the side of a pencil eraser or a large straw.

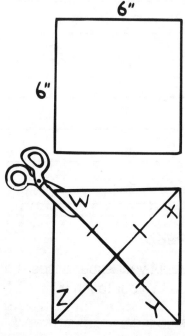

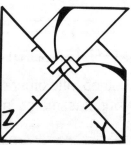

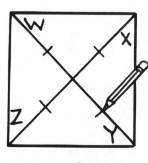

NAME _____

MAKING PINWHEELS

TESTING THE PINWHEEL

1. Take the pinwheel outside and hold it up into the air to see if the wind catches the loops and makes it whirl around.

2. Try running so that a moving stream of air created by your movement catches the loops of the pinwheel and makes them whirl.

3. Try standing in one place and slowly moving the pinwheel through the air in different directions.

4. Which of the three activities worked best for you today? Check the box for your choice.

| HOLDING IT | RUNNING WITH IT | MOVING IT SLOWLY |

Why? What were the wind conditions? _____

_____

5. Use arrows to draw the direction of the wind towards your pinwheel in the box you checked that worked the best.

PINWHEEL ACTIVITIES

1. Work with a partner to try to get both of your pinwheels to move at the same time and speed. If the wind is not blowing, use a fan or a hair dryer.

   Try different methods such as holding them side-by-side or back-to-back.

   Which method worked best? _____

2. Try blowing on the wheels at the same time. Can you and your partner get both wheels moving at the same time and speed?   **YES   NO**

   How did you do it? _____

   _____

3. Use four different-colored markers to draw on the four sections of the pinwheel. Put the pinwheels in motion in the wind or with a fan. Be careful not to flatten or fold the loops.

   What happens to the designs when the pinwheel is in motion? _____

   _____

MAKING PINWHEELS

JOURNAL ENTRY

1. Describe which method of moving the pinwheel worked best for you. _____

   _____

   _____

   _____

2. What method worked best, when working with a partner, to get both wheels moving at the same speed?

   _____

   _____

   _____

3. Draw the wind blowing your pinwheel in the frame:

4. Which direction did you get the wind blowing your pinwheel to make it work the best?

   IN FRONT   BEHIND   ON THE SIDE   ABOVE

5. What ideas did you get about making a pinwheel of your own design?

   _____

   _____

   _____

DESIGN PROCESS REVIEW—MAKING PINWHEELS

Share your observations, journal entries, and other documentation about your experiences in building and using your pinwheel with your classmates in a discussion led by your teacher.

WIND WHEELS

Teacher Preparation: Plan this activity for a windy day/week. If there is no wind available, use electric fans or hair dryers. The straight straws used should not be as long as the barbeque skewers. You may need to cut the straws prior to the activity.

TEAM MATERIALS
- construction paper or manila folders
- masking tape and clear tape
- pushpins
- straight drinking straws
- rulers
- scissors
- timer or stopwatch
- water bottles with caps
- wooden barbeque skewers

Optional: electric fans or hair dryers

Directions: Work with a partner. Each partner can measure, cut, and fold one square wheel. Then, work together to combine them and assemble the wind wheel.

MAKING THE TWO WHEELS

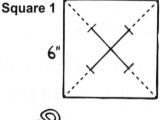

1. Measure, draw, and cut out two 6" squares using heavy paper.
2. Draw 2 diagonal lines from opposite corners to divide the squares into 4 equal triangles.
3. From each outside corner, measure in 3" and mark it. Do this for both squares.
4. Then, cut 3" in from each corner of the squares, along the diagonal lines.
5. **Square 1:** Fold each small triangle until the fold makes a right angle. To do this, fold the left corner towards the center.
6. **Square 2:** Fold the right side of the small triangles towards the center.
7. Hold the two wheels back-to-back. The four cut "fins" should be folded in opposite directions.

ASSEMBLING THE WIND WHEEL

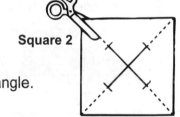

1. Fill an empty water bottle with water and twist the cap back on. This will provide a solid base for the wind wheel.
2. Lay a plastic drinking straw on the cap. Center it and tape it down.
3. Slide a thin, wooden skewer through the straw. It should slide in easily. It will extend in both directions past the straw.
4. Use a pushpin to make a small hole in the center of each of the wheels. Wiggle the pushpin to make the hole large enough to stick the first wheel onto the sharp end of the skewer.
5. Enlarge the hole in the other wheel and slide it over the other end of the skewer. This one will take a bit more effort since the end is not pointed.
6. Firmly attach both wheels to the skewer with clear tape. Don't get tape on the straw, just the skewer.

WIND WHEELS

Directions: Work with your partner to test the wind wheel you made. Take turns timing.

TESTING YOUR WIND WHEEL

1. Arrange your wind wheel on the playground or an outside table. Stabilize it with tape if you need to. Try to find a place where the wind is not blocked by structures or trees. The higher up you can place the wind wheel, the easier it will be to catch the wind. Observe.

2. Did the wind wheel spin around smoothly?   **YES   NO**

   Describe its movement. _____

3. Did you need to adjust it in some way?   **YES   NO**

   What did you do? _____

4. How fast did your wind wheel move? _____

5. Did you notice other students' wind wheels moving differently?   **YES   NO**

   If so, what differences did you observe? _____

6. Try to compute how many turns the wheel makes in 10 seconds, 30 seconds, and 1 minute. Record your results in the column for **Trial 1**.

HOW MANY TURNS		
TIME	TRIAL 1	TRIAL 2
10 SECONDS		
30 SECONDS		
60 SECONDS		

7. Modify your wind wheel as needed. Then, run the three timed-tests again. Record your times in the column for **Trial 2**.

8. Review your data and compare results from the first and second trial. What did you observe?

_____

WIND WHEELS

Directions: After you have tested and timed the wind wheel twice, see if you can improve the design even more.

MODIFY YOUR WIND WHEEL

1. Plan a model with your partner. Decide what to make. You may work on one modification or each do a separate version.

   Consider one of these modifications when designing your wind wheel:

   - use circular wheels with more folds or larger folds
   - use larger wheels or different-styled wheels
   - use triangular wheels
   - cut more than 4 "blades"

2. Sketch your plan in the space to the right.

3. Describe the model you are developing. Explain the improvements.

   _____

   _____

   _____

   _____

TEST YOUR MODIFIED WHEEL

1. Place your wind wheel on the patio, playground, or outside table, or hold it up, aiming it into the wind.

2. Describe how it worked and how fast it moved. _____

   _____

3. Try to compute how many turns the wheel makes in 10 seconds, 30 seconds, and 1 minute.

10 SEC.	30 SEC.	60 SEC.

4. What modification (change) might have worked better? _____

   _____

   Why? _____

WIND WHEELS

JOURNAL ENTRY

1. Describe how your first wind wheel worked. _____

   _____

   _____

   _____

2. What changes and improvements to the first model did you make?

   _____

   _____

   _____

3. Did the modifications you made work well?   **YES**   **NO**

   Explain. _____

   _____

   _____

   _____

4. What modifications would you make if you were to design and build a new wind wheel?

   _____

   _____

   _____

5. What uses can you think of for your wind wheel?

   _____

   _____

   _____

DESIGN PROCESS REVIEW—WIND WHEELS

Share your observations, journal entries, and other documentation about your wind wheel activities with your classmates in a discussion led by your teacher.

ⓃⒶⓂⒺ _____

CHALLENGE: DESIGN YOUR OWN WIND DEVICE

Directions: Use the steps in the Design Process to make a new wind indicator device, toy, or tool.

BRAINSTORM: Think about the different types of wind indicators you have already made in this unit. Review any modifications you tried or observed.

What modifications did you observe in your creations, or those of your fellow students, that worked well?

_____

_____

What problems did you experience or observe? _____

_____

_____

What would you like to try now? _____

_____

_____

What research will you do? _____

_____

_____

DESIGN THE SOLUTION: Describe what you plan to make and how you plan to accomplish your goal.

_____

_____

Sketch your ideas here. Add notes.

_____

_____

_____

_____

_____

_____

_____

_____

NAME _____

CHALLENGE: DESIGN YOUR OWN WIND DEVICE

BUILD: Create your own wind indicator using a design and size of your choosing. Keep a record of the measurements you used. Use materials provided in previous activities or request permission to add a new material for your invention. Your additional materials might include paper cups or plates. Sketch your plan in the space to the right.

MATERIALS AND MEASUREMENTS

_____

_____

_____

_____

EVALUATE: Does your wind device work?   **YES   NO**

Explain how it works or why it does not work. _____

_____

_____

MODIFY: Did you make modifications?   **YES   NO**

If modifications were made on your wind device, describe them. _____

_____

SHARE: What do you call your device? _____

What does your device do? _____

_____

Would this device be useful if sold in stores?   **YES   NO**

Explain. _____

_____

What surprised you the most about this activity? _____

_____

What would you do if you could make another device? _____

_____

UNIT 6

MOTION AND MOMENTUM

> **3 sessions:** 1 session for each activity (approximately 1 to $1\frac{1}{2}$ hours per session)

Focus: Physical Science—motion, momentum, friction

CONNECTIONS AND SUGGESTIONS

SCIENCE—Motion involves movement. It may be circular, linear, curved, or go in many different directions. Students will use marbles of different sizes and weights to study linear momentum—objects moving in straight lines. Students will vary the angles of foam runways to study how different heights (angles) affect momentum.

TECHNOLOGY—Students may use computers or personal tablets to do research on motion and momentum. Additionally, they can photograph their observations and responses as they record information, write journal entries, and prepare reports. A variety of items will be used to record times and speeds such as stopwatches and calculators.

ENGINEERING—Students will work using the design method to assemble an apparatus to construct runways for marbles using foam insulation tubing. They will also design roller coaster tracks with loop-de-loops by connecting lengths of the tubing. In working with elements of design they will try to build longer and more complex roller coasters and observe momentum by varying the heights of the runways and the weights of the marbles.

MATH—Students may use rulers to measure heights and distances and they may use calculators to compare speeds and distances. Graphs or charts can be formulated to compare speeds over different courses.

DISCUSSION PROMPT: What Is Momentum?

Momentum is the impetus or power of a moving object. Two things create momentum:

— the *mass* of an object, which is the amount of material in an object (Students in this unit will use marbles.)

— the *velocity* or speed of a moving object in one direction

In simple terms, momentum is affected by how big an object is and how fast it is moving. The momentum of an object is influenced by its mass, its shape (round works best), the friction of the object it is moving on, and the force applied to put it in motion. Momentum is never really created or destroyed in a closed system like the universe. This is because energy is neither created or destroyed. However, the momentum of a particular object, such as a boulder in motion, does slow and will eventually stop due to the friction of the ground.

* To generate enthusiasm, you may wish to share the following take on momentum.
Momentum in Rube Goldberg machines: *https://www.youtube.com/watch?v=Hytq-yTqwdc*

MOTION AND MOMENTUM

UNIT MATERIALS (for a class of 30 to 35)

- ☐ 8–12 oz. paper or plastic cups
- ☐ foam pipe insulation tubes*
- ☐ cardboard tubes and boxes
- ☐ large marbles
- ☐ regular marbles
- ☐ masking tape
- ☐ rulers and tape measures or yard sticks
- ☐ scissors

*Teacher Preparation: Use $\frac{3}{4}$ inch foam insulation tubes from a hardware store. Prior to the activity, slice the tubes lengthwise using a serrated knife. *Note:* Do not use stiff "pool noodles." Although readily available, they are not generally pliable enough to create the roller coaster loop-de-loops that are incorporated into Activity 2 and the final challenge.

NOTES

_____

_____

_____

_____

_____

_____

_____

_____

_____

_____

_____

_____

FIND OUT MORE

Annenberg Learner Interactives—Amusement Park Physics
Scroll down and go to: Design a Roller Coaster
http://www.learner.org/interactives/parkphysics/coaster.html

Museum of Science and Industry—Build a Roller Coaster
http://www.msichicago.org/online-science/activities/activity-detail/type/print/activities/build-a-roller-coaster/

4-H science leader teaches the marble roller coaster experiment
https://www.youtube.com/watch?v=1GZEOjVLEXQ

Marble Roller Coasters 2011
https://www.youtube.com/watch?v=MrUKVSAoU7s

Safety Note: All websites should be checked prior to student viewing to be certain that content is appropriate.

MOTION AND MOMENTUM VOCABULARY

<u>circular</u>—in a circle

<u>kinetic energy</u>—energy from motion
Example: a marble rolling down a hill

<u>friction</u>—the rubbing of one surface or object against another; friction is the force that resists the motion and slows an object down. For example,

— Hands rubbing together get warm due to friction.

— The speed of a marble rolling down a ramp is affected by how smooth the ramp is.

<u>linear</u>—in a straight line

<u>mass</u>—the quantity of matter that a body contains

<u>momentum</u>—the force of a moving object

<u>motion</u>—the process of movement

<u>potential energy</u>—stored energy that changes into kinetic energy
Example: a marble resting at the top of a hill has stored energy that is waiting to be released when it rolls down the hill

<u>velocity</u>—a measurement of the rate and direction an object travels

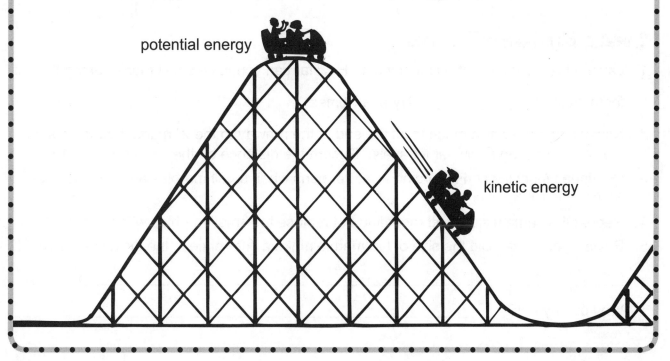

potential energy

kinetic energy

MARBLE RUNWAYS

Directions: Work in groups of two or three to create marble runways to observe linear momentum. Test the runways at different heights. Take turns launching the marble, lifting the foam runway, and measuring and recording where the marble lands.

TEAM MATERIALS

- foam insulation tubes
- marbles—small and large
- rulers
- masking tape
- small paper or plastic cups
- tape measures or yard sticks

MARBLE RUNWAY—ASSEMBLY

1. Use one half of a foam insulation tube to create a marble runway. Place the tube on a long table or several connected desks.

2. Tape a ruler upright on the desk near one end of the foam tube. This will be the starting point for all marbles.

3. Tape a small cup securely to the other end of the foam tube. It should catch the marble(s) at the end of the roll.

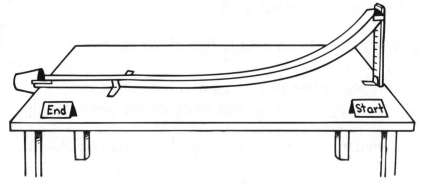

MARBLE RUNWAY—TESTING

1. Lay the foam runway flat and test it out. How far can you roll a small marble along the flat, foam channel? _____ Try a few times.

2. Now use the ruler as a guide to lift the end of the runway to the 2" mark. Launch a small marble and observe how far it travels. Record the distance on the chart on page 153.

3. Continue launching and recording what happens when small marbles are launched at 4", 6", 8", and 10" heights.

4. Repeat the same testing and recording but replace the small marbles with large marbles.

5. Review your data. Did the size of the marble make a difference in the distances traveled?

_____

Why or why not? _____

_____

NAME _____

MARBLE RUNWAYS

MARBLE RUNWAY—TESTING

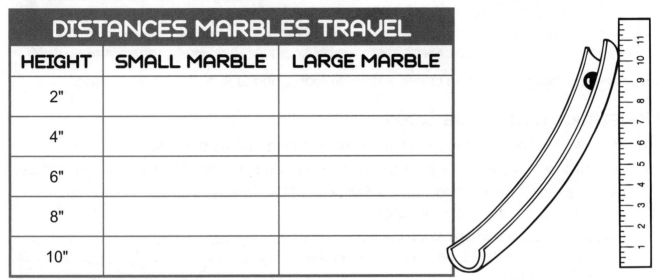

DISTANCES MARBLES TRAVEL		
HEIGHT	SMALL MARBLE	LARGE MARBLE
2"		
4"		
6"		
8"		
10"		

ADD MORE MARBLES—TEST MOMENTUM

1. Raise the slide of the runway to a height of 10".

2. Place one marble halfway down the runway (on the flat part). That will be the "sitting" marble.

3. Launch a second marble, the striker, from the top of the slide.

4. What happens to the "sitting" marble when it is hit by the striker? _____

_____

5. Place two marbles halfway down a runway and launch the striker. What happens to the two sitting marbles?

_____

VARY THE SIZE OF THE MARBLES—TEST MOMENTUM

1. Observe linear momentum using the set-ups below for the sitting marbles. **S** represents a small marble and **L** represents a large marble.

2. Describe what happens to each group of marbles when hit by the striker.

   _____

  _____

   _____

LOOP-DE-LOOPS

TEAM MATERIALS
- foam insulation tubes
- marbles—small and large
- rulers
- masking tape
- small paper or plastic cups
- tape measures or yard sticks

Directions: Work as a team to create a loop-de-loop using tape and the foam tubing.

CONSTRUCT A LOOP-DE-LOOP

1. Tape two sections of tubing together to create a long runway or track.

2. Determine which end will be the start and attach a cup to the other end to catch the marbles.

3. Decide if one partner will hold up the Start end of the runway to launch the marble or if you will tape it to a wall or other area.

4. Create a loop somewhere along the longer runway. Use tape to secure the loop but don't cover the channel in the track.

TEST THE LOOP-DE-LOOP

1. Launch a small marble from the starting point of your runway to test the loop-de-loop.

   Did the marble complete the loop-de-loop and land in the cup?   **YES   NO**

   If not, keep trying until the marble can get enough momentum to complete the loop and travel to the cup. Try adjusting the starting height or the size of the loop. What did you need to do?

   _____

2. Take measurements once your marble successfully makes the loop-de-loop and lands in the cup.

   What is the diameter of the loop-de-loop? _____

   At what height did you launch the marbles? _____

3. Try launching a different size marble. Does it work as well as the first marble?   **YES   NO**

   Explain. _____

   _____

4. Discuss your findings. What was the most important thing you learned about momentum in creating a loop-de-loop?

   _____

 _____

MARBLE RUNWAYS AND LOOP-DE-LOOPS

JOURNAL ENTRY

1. How does the angle of the runway affect a marble rolling down?

   _____

   _____

2. Which angles or heights were best for moving a marble through a loop-de-loop?

   _____

   _____

3. What happened when a striker hit a sitting marble? _____

   _____

   _____

4. What happened when a striker hit a group of sitting marbles? _____

   _____

   _____

5. What conclusions could you draw about the movement of the marbles after completing the two activities?

   _____

   _____

   _____

6. What surprised you the most about this experiment with marbles and runways?

   _____

   _____

   _____

DESIGN REVIEW PROCESS—MARBLE RUNWAYS AND LOOP-DE-LOOPS

Share your information and conclusions in the general discussion moderated by your teacher. Make sure that you have at least one serious idea, observation, or reaction to contribute. Be a willing contributor to the discussion as well as a careful listener.

CHALLENGE: DESIGN A ROLLER COASTER

Directions: Combine with another team to create a unique, working roller coaster that carries marbles along a course and brings them to a final stopping place. Include high and low areas, loops and hills. You may add other materials such as boxes, books, or paper towel tubes with teacher approval.

BRAINSTORM: Think about what you have learned about *linear momentum*, and *potential* and *kinetic energy*.

How can you use that information to create a roller coaster with enough kinetic energy at the beginning to allow a marble to travel down a slope and all the way to the end?

_____

_____

What kind of research do you need to do?

_____

_____

DESIGN THE SOLUTION: Sketch your plans here. Think of the space you have to work in. Will you add other materials to your roller coaster? Consider arranging your roller coaster tubes on tables, along coat hooks, from poles, in hallways, along walls, on shelves or cabinets, etc. Add notes.

_____

_____

_____

_____

CHALLENGE: DESIGN A ROLLER COASTER

BUILD: Construct your roller coaster using materials from previous activities and additional approved materials. List all your materials here.

_____   _____   _____

_____   _____   _____

Describe materials you created or used for supports on your roller coaster.

_____

_____

EVALUATE: What was the most interesting part of the construction process?

_____

_____

Did your original design work as planned?   **YES   NO**

Explain. _____

_____

_____

MODIFY: What adjustments would you like to make to improve your roller coaster? List them and sketch your plan below.

ADJUSTMENTS: _____

_____

SHARE: Describe the results of your project. _____

_____

Do you think you would like to design roller coasters and other rides as a career? **YES NO**

Explain. _____

Common Core State Standards

Each lesson meets one or more of the following Common Core State Standards © Copyright 2010. National Governors Association Center for Best Practices and Council of Chief State School Officers. All rights reserved. For more information about the Common Core State Standards, go to *http://www.corestandards.org/* or *http://www.teachercreated.com/standards*.

Reading Informational Text Standards	Activity	Page	Activity	Page
Key Ideas and Details				
ELA.RI.4.1 Refer to details and examples in a text when explaining what the text says explicitly and when drawing inferences from the text.	Unit 1—Centripetal Force Unit 2—Pendulums Unit 3—Soap Science	23–46 50–74 78–102	Unit 4—Surface Tension Unit 5—The Power of Wind Unit 6—Motion and Momentum	105–128 131–148 152–157

ELA.RI.4.3 Explain events, procedures, ideas, or concepts in a historical, scientific, or technical text, including what happened and why, based on specific information in the text.	Unit 1—Centripetal Force
	Unit 1—Newton's Laws of Motion
	Unit 1—Lifting Spinners
	Unit 1—Planetary Spinners
	Unit 1—Water-Cup Spinners
	Unit 1—Centripetal Water Spinners
	Unit 1—Spinner Speeds
	Unit 1—Challenge: Design a Spinner
	Unit 2—Pendulums
	Unit 2—What Is a Pendulum?
	Unit 2—Make a Simple Pendulum
	Unit 2—Angles and Oscillations
	Unit 2—Working with Two Pendulums
	Unit 2—Challenge: Create a Pendulum Wave
	Unit 3—Soap Science
	Unit 3—Creating soap Bubbles
	Unit 3—2D-Shape Wands
	Unit 3—3D-Shape Wands
	Unit 3—Flexible Bubble Wands
		23
		24
		25–31
		32–34
		35–37
		38–39
		40–44
		45–46
		50
		51
		52–60
		61–67
		68–71
		72–74
		78–82
		83–87
		88–93
		94–97
		98–100
			Unit 3—Challenge: Make Super Bubbles
			Unit 4—Surface Tension
			Unit 4—Coin Meniscus
			Unit 4—Cup Meniscus
			Unit 4—Moving Boats
			Unit 4—Floating Clips
			Unit 4—Challenge: Be a Chemist—
			      Find the Fastest Fuel
			Unit 5—The Power of Wind
			Unit 5—Wind Direction
			Unit 5—Measuring Wind Speed
			Unit 5—Making Pinwheels
			Unit 5—Wind Wheels
			Unit 5—Challenge: Design Your Own
			      Wind Device
			Unit 6—Marble Runways
			Unit 6—Loop-De-Loops
			Unit 6—Marble Runways and Loop-De-Loops
			Unit 6—Challenge: Design a Roller Coaster
				101–102
				106–108
				109–113
				114–116
				117–120
				121–125
				
				126–128
				132
				133–136
				137–139
				140–142
				143–146
				
				147–148
				152–153
				154
				155
				156–157

Craft and Structure				
ELA.RI.4.4 Determine the meaning of general academic and domain-specific words or phrases in a text relevant to a grade 4 topic or subject area.	Unit 1—Centripetal Force Vocabulary Unit 2—Pendulums Vocabulary Unit 3—Soap Science Vocabulary Unit 3—Soap Science	22 49 77 81	Unit 4—Surface Tension Vocabulary Unit 5—The Power of Wind Vocabulary Unit 6—Motion and Momentum Vocabulary	105 131 151
ELA.RI.4.5 Describe the overall structure (e.g., chronology, comparison, cause/effect, problem/solution) of events, ideas, concepts, or information in a text or part of a text.	Unit 1—Centripetal Force Unit 2—Pendulums Unit 3—Soap Science	23–46 50–74 78–102	Unit 4—Surface Tension Unit 5—The Power of Wind Unit 6—Motion and Momentum	105–128 131–148 152–157
Integration of Knowledge and Ideas				
ELA.RI.4.7 Interpret information presented visually, orally, or quantitatively (e.g., in charts, graphs, diagrams, time lines, animations, or interactive elements on Web pages) and explain how the information contributes to an understanding of the text in which it appears.	Unit 1—Centripetal Force Unit 2—Pendulums Unit 3—Soap Science Unit 4—Surface Tension Unit 5—The Power of Wind Unit 6—Motion and Momentum	23–46 50–74 78–102 105–128 131–148 152–157		
Range of Reading and Level of Text Complexity				
ELA.RI.4.10 By the end of year, read and comprehend informational texts, including history/social studies, science, and technical texts, in the grades 4–5 text complexity band proficiently, with scaffolding as needed at the high end of the range.	Unit 1—Centripetal Force Unit 2—Pendulums Unit 3—Soap Science Unit 4—Surface Tension Unit 5—The Power of Wind Unit 6—Motion and Momentum	23–46 50–74 78–102 105–128 131–148 152–157		